THE LITTLE BOOK OF ANIMAL REIKI

A Beginner's Guide to Energy Healing for Pets and Animals

By Harriette-Rose and Molly Malone

Copyright © 2020 by Harriette-Rose and Molly Malone | All Rights Reserved

No part of this publication may be reproduced, stored in a retrieval system, or transmitted in any form or by any means, electronic, mechanical, photocopying, recording, scanning, or otherwise, without prior written permission of the Publisher. Requests to the Publisher for permission should be addressed via the online contact form at https://www.reiki-store.com/contact. Unauthorized reproduction of any part of this work is illegal and punishable by law.

License: Personal Use Only

For More Information about Reiki and our certified Animal Reiki Home Study Course please visit: www.reiki-store.com

AUTHORS AND PUBLISHERS DISCLAIMER

Reiki is an ancient form of healing that is practiced by numerous practitioners around the world in order to help relax people and animals. The information and techniques in this book do not constitute medical advice. Energy healing and medicine are two very different disciplines. You should always seek medical advice from a qualified vet or medical practitioner if you believe an animal to be unwell. While all suggested treatments are offered in good faith, the author and publisher cannot accept responsibility for the health, wellbeing and happiness of an animals or any illness arising out of the failure of the reader/individual to seek medical advice from a qualified doctor, vet or medical practitioner. Reiki should always only be used in conjunction with veterinary medicine, not in place of veterinary medicine or advice. Practitioners of Reiki do not diagnose medical conditions, nor do they prescribe, perform medical treatment, or interfere with the treatment of a licensed medical professional. We cannot accept any responsibility for your own health and safety whilst you are practicing animal Reiki, you should always use your own judgement when working with an animal, and get the necessary legal protection and recognized certification to practice safely in your area.

IMPORTANT NOTE TO THE READER

This book is for educational purposes only. If you desire to use the teachings contained within this book to practice Reiki on your pets and other animals, you must first have received the necessary Reiki attunements from a Reiki Master either in person or via distant reiki attunement.

If you would like to find out more about Reiki Distant Attunements and Animal Reiki Master Teacher Certification, please check out our website: www.reiki-store.com. In different countries and states, there will be different legal requirements for practicing Reiki on animals professionally, it is your responsibility to check and abide by the laws regulating Reiki Practitioners in your local area and obtain the necessary insurance to protect you before you get started.

OUR REIKI LINEAGE

Dr Mikao Usui
Dr Chujiro Hayashi
Madam Hawayo Takata
Iris Ishikura
Arthur Robertson
Rick & Emma Ferguson
Margarette L Shelton
Kathleen Ann Milner
Robert N Wachsberger
Tricia Courtney-Dickens
Adele and Garry Malone
Harriette-Rose and Molly Malone

"

ANIMAL LOVERS ARE A SPECIAL BREED OF HUMANS, GENEROUS OF SPIRIT, FULL OF EMPATHY...WITH HEARTS AS BIG AS A CLOUDLESS SKY." - JOHN GROGAN, AUTHOR OF MARLEY & ME

TABLE OF CONTENTS

Introduction   1
Before you get Started   3
What are the Benefits of Animal Reiki?   5
What is Reiki?   7
Origins of Reiki   10
The Five Principles of Reiki   15
How do we Connect to Reiki?   17
Why is Reiki Ideal for treating Animals?   19
How Does Reiki Work?   22
Auras in Animals   25
The Energy Centres in Animals   28
What Happens During an Animal Reiki Session?   33
Important Considerations when Treating an Animal with Reiki   38
How to Start an Animal Reiki Session   45
Understanding the Signs that an Animals is Accepting Reiki   52
Using Hand Positions during an Animal Reiki Session   55
How do you know when to End an Animal Reiki Session?   63
Different Animals will have Different Needs   66
    Reiki with Dogs   67
    Reiki with Cats   69
    Reiki with Birds   71
    Reiki with Horses   74
    Reiki with Other Small Animals   76
Good luck on your Reiki Journey   79
About The Reiki Store   81

INTRODUCTION

"Until one has loved an animal, a part of one's soul remains unawakened."- Anatole France

Having a pet is one of the most beautiful gifts. They teach us about trust, companionship and unconditional love. They are our best friends and family members, our loyal confidantes and supporters. Even after a busy and chaotic day, having a pet means always going home to a friendly face.

If you have pets, you'll know how quickly they pick up on the emotions of the humans they live with. Have you ever, for example, noticed how a pet will approach you if you are feeling a bit down or sad? They are emotional beings and sense when things are wrong and undoubtedly experience happiness, joy, excitement, sadness, fear, anxiety, jealousy and anger as we do.

In fact, animals are very sensitive to energy, which is why energy therapies like Reiki work really well with animals. Animal Reiki is becoming an increasingly popular way to work with and enhance the lives of pets and animals as a result, using Reiki energy to harness the body's innate energetic ability to heal and re-balance.

As the costs of looking after our pets continues to rise, the beautiful thing about Reiki is that it is a safe and natural healing therapy that is easy to learn and simple to administer at home. It works wonderfully in conjunction with other medical treatments, diets and procedures to promote health and wellbeing every day.

The purpose of this book is to give you a comprehensive introduction to the teachings and methods associated with hands-on Reiki for pets and animals – where we use our hands to channel Reiki energy to the animals that we know well and are comfortable working with. We have purposely kept the information concise, so anyone can learn how Reiki can be used to help the animals they care for, regardless of their previous experience with Reiki. We will be demystifying how Reiki works, and jargon-busting, to fast-track your knowledge of this powerful tool for self-care and energy health. We hope this information will be of equal benefit to those with a new curiosity for animal Reiki and those who have already experienced some of its benefits, acting as a handy go-to guide whenever you are in need of some inspiration or a quick Reiki refresher!

Overall, we hope that this book inspires more people to practice animal Reiki, equipping pet-owners and animal lovers alike with new skills to help care for the animals in their lives. Hopefully this book is just one step on a much bigger journey with Reiki and we are very grateful to be a part of that Reiki journey!

BEFORE YOU GET STARTED

"When I look into the eyes of an animal, I do not see an animal. I see a living being. I see a friend. I feel a soul." - Anthony Douglas Williams

People from all walks of life are drawn to animal Reiki for many different reasons. We have been practicing animal Reiki and training students for many years, and find that many of our students stumble upon Reiki whilst searching for natural ways to support the health needs of their pets, especially when they are experiencing health problems or issues with stress and anxiety at home. It's great to see these Reiki-newbies leaving as Reiki enthusiasts and advocates, with a deeper connection to their pets and new skills to care for them each day!

Certainly, whatever your experience level with Reiki, the secret to getting the most from this ancient energy technique and this book in fact, is to be completely open to the possibilities of Reiki. This means leaving any skepticism or doubts at the door. Even if there are things you don't understand, take comfort in the fact that Reiki works, even if you don't understand it – there are indeed a lot of things in life that we might not fully understand the detailed ins and outs of, but we can still trust that they are working!

Reiki comes from a higher source, but it is important to understand that different people will have different beliefs about what this higher source is – a God, the Universe, a powerful energy, spirit, a creator or higher power or equally something unknown or undefined. We welcome you to incorporate your own beliefs when working through this book – Reiki is not a religion and is compatible with all religious belief systems. It is based upon universal principles of gratitude, love and honesty – which create a positive spiritual connection between humans and all living things. You can receive Reiki and practice this healing system whatever your religion or faith.

There are a few more really important things to note before we get started. The first thing is that this book is an educational tool for anyone interested in using Reiki with animals. We hope that it will inspire you to learn more and take the next steps to practice Reiki on your own pets or professionally on other animal clients - receiving the necessary Reiki attunements (the initiation ceremony for Reiki that unlocks your energy potential), and carrying out the necessary training to become a certified Animal Reiki Practitioner. If you are just looking to practice Reiki on your pets at home you don't have to get certified, but you will need to be attuned to Reiki. You can find out more about Reiki attunements at www.reiki-store.com.

It's also important to note here that the information and techniques in this book should never be a substitute for medical advice from a trained vet. You should always seek medical advice from a qualified vet if you believe that an animal is unwell and speak to your vet before you begin any Reiki sessions on your pet. Of course, if you are working on an animal that is not your own, you should always speak to the owner to gain their permission to work with their animal, making sure they are aware of what is involved in a Reiki session, and that they have in turn spoken to their vet ahead of a session.

Now let's get started!

WHAT ARE THE BENEFITS OF ANIMAL REIKI?

"Eventually you will come to understand that love heals everything, and love is all there is." - Gary Zukav

You may have experienced some the incredible benefits of a Reiki treatment yourself – such as intense relaxation, pain relief and help with the symptoms of an illness or ailment. When working with animals, we expect similar benefits. Naturally, every animal will be different and have unique life experiences, issues and species-specific health complications that may need attention, but the incredible thing about Reiki is that whatever the problem, Reiki energy goes where it is needed to do the greatest good (which is pretty helpful when animals cannot verbalize specific issues or complaints!)

Whilst some benefits of a Reiki session may be visible immediately such as having a relaxing and calming effect on a stressed or poorly animal, other benefits may not be visibly noticeable or take several sessions to manifest. It's the same as a course of antibiotics –you have to finish the whole course to get the desired outcome.

Some of the powerful ways in which Animal Reiki can help our animal friends are noted below. Reiki energy:

- Can provide relaxation in stressful situations – for example visiting the vet, travelling in a car, or when introducing an animal into a new environment.
- Can accelerate and support healing following surgery, illness or injury.
- Can provide pain relief
- Can help keep a healthy animal well – boosting their natural immunity
- Can help with behavioral problems and emotional issues like separation anxiety or nervousness around new people.
- Naturally boost the effects of traditional medicines and treatments.
- Improve the relationships we have with our pets – as we surround them in loving Reiki energy and feel more connected to them.
- Help a grieving animal if their owners have passed.
- Provide support for pregnant animals throughout their pregnancy, especially if they are a first-time parent.
- Provide support for very sick or dying animals and their owners, improving the quality of life in the time they have left, by healing pain, fear and suffering.
- Reiki can be beneficial to us too! The more we channel Reiki, the more we surround ourselves with its healing energies, enhancing our own health and wellbeing.

WHAT IS REIKI?

"When you're at peace with your life and in a state of tranquillity, you actually send out a vibration of energy that impacts all living creatures, including plants, animals." ~ Wayne Dyer

Every living thing in the universe is delicately made up of and connected by energy. Reiki is an ancient Japanese healing technique, that harnesses and harmonizes this powerful life-giving energy that flows through everyone and everything to promote stress-reduction, relaxation and improve wellbeing. By placing our hands over the body, we can channel this invisible energy from the universe through our hands to balance the energy in the person or animal we are working with for positive benefits.

Reiki, pronounced RAY-KEY, is a two syllable Japanese word meaning 'Universal Life Force.'

'Rei' means higher power, universal or omnipresent – present everywhere at the same time. This acknowledges the fact that Reiki energy comes from a higher source, a source outside ourselves. This means that Reiki cannot be depleted. You can practice Reiki your whole life and never deplete your own energy stores because you are channeling energy from an unlimited source in the universe.

'Ki' means life force energy. It is the energy that gives life to all living things. It is also known as Chi by the Chinese, Prana by a number of Asian cultures and the Holy Spirit or Holy Ghost by most of the Western world. All living things carry this life-giving energy in and around our bodies from the moment we are conceived.

Rei - Universal

When you feel healthy and full of life, the flow of Ki energy in the body is high. You are able to respond to the highs and lows of life with resilience and perspective - your immune system is strong, and you have a higher resistance to illness and disease.

Ki - Life Force

However, when the flow of Ki energy is blocked or weakened, due to factors like stress, substance abuse, lack of sleep, malnourishment, loneliness, abuse and neglect or physical injury, the balance of energy in the body is disturbed and you are more susceptible to disease and sickness. You will find it difficult to deal with life's challenges.

We are all born with the natural ability to stimulate balance and healing in our internal systems to support everyday life – our wounds heal, our bodies regulate a myriad of cell reactions and processes to keep order, and fight infections by seeking out and eliminating foreign invaders. Have you ever stopped to consider why, if we get hurt or injured, we intuitively place our hand on the sore spot to relieve the pain? Or thought about why we instinctively place a comforting hand on our loved ones when they are sad or upset? This is Reiki energy at work – a positive exchange of energy to relieve pain and promote relaxation! Whilst our early ancestors used and relied on these intuitive instincts and innate healing abilities to thrive and stay well, modern humanity has increasingly lost touch with these ancient natural ways, relying heavily on modern drugs and medicinal fixes. We have become disconnected from the Reiki which is ever-present in our bodies.

Fortunately, many disciplines such as Reiki, Tai Chi, Feng Shui, Martial Arts, Meditation, Yoga and Acupuncture have all been developed to activate the universal Ki energy and greatly enhance the flow of this energy in and around the body to maintain health. Acupuncture for example uses needles to clear energy blockages, whilst Feng Shui is a discipline based on balancing the flow of energy around a space to benefit those that live there.

Reiki healing recognizes that we are all energy beings with physical, mental, emotional and spiritual needs which each have their own energy properties. Instead of just treating a physical symptom or issue like traditional medicine, Reiki looks to seek out the origin of the imbalance and treat the person as a whole – mind, body and soul. It works to harmonize any blockages and imbalances in the flow of energy through our bodies and the energy fields that surround us, in order to stimulate our body's natural healing abilities.

Crucially, it is important to note that when you practice animal Reiki, you are not healing your pets and animals, the animal receiving Reiki is in fact healing themselves. You are merely the channel for the Universal Life Force. You enable the animal to draw the Reiki energy they require through you, to heal on a deep and natural level. Reiki relies on the wisdom of the body to know what it requires – naturally seeking out imbalances to restore energetic equilibrium. As Reiki is drawn from the universe and not sent, the amount of energy drawn during a session will depend on the needs of the person or animal receiving it.

Reiki is never used to substitute medical treatments and medicines. It is a powerful complementary medicine, which means that it can work alongside conventional medicine, to improve health and general wellbeing.

Reiki is not a mysterious or complicated system that only a few privileged people can access. It is not a practice of secrets and rules and you can't get Reiki wrong. The skills and techniques associated with Reiki are simple and easy to learn so you can channel healing energy to your pets and the animals you care for. What is crucial is the intention to help the animal, Reiki energy will seek out the imbalances and do the rest!

Undoubtedly, Reiki is a special gift and should always be respected and treated as such. In a noisy, demanding and stressful world, Reiki energy can promote wellness, peace, relaxation and balance, helping the animals we love and care for to thrive, and we should always remain grateful of this gift.

ORIGINS OF REIKI

"Each of us has the potential of being given a gift by the divine, which results in the body and soul becoming unified ... Through it, the human being will first be made healthy, and then peace of mind and joy in life will be increased." - Dr Mikao Usui

The history of Reiki is believed to go back many centuries although it's hard to pinpoint its exact birth. Some believe that the lost civilizations of Mu and Atlantis developed these techniques to harness the Universal Life Force. Others believe that Reiki was first performed by Buddha and Jesus. We know that many ancient cultures passed their beliefs, stories and practices down to the next generation through word of mouth, rather than the written word, so it is indeed possible that Reiki has been practiced for millennia and it simply hasn't been documented. We are however able to pinpoint the start of the modern history of Reiki. This begins at the end of the nineteenth century when Reiki was rediscovered by Dr Mikao Usui (1865-1926).

DR MIKAO USUI

Mikao Usui was born into a family in southern Japan that had been practicing Zen Buddhism for eleven generations. He complemented his knowledge of meditation and scriptures, with the study of modern medicine and science.

When a cholera epidemic spread through Tokyo, Usui was struck down with the disease. During his hospitalization, as he was close to death, he had a spiritual experience. This inspired Usui to study the ancient teachings of his ancestors. He joined a Zen monastery and began reading the ancient Sanskrit and Sutras (ancient religious manuals and texts).

After many years of study Usui found references to an ancient form of healing. Further study revealed methods, formulas and symbols that detailed exactly how to practice and master this art of hands on healing. However, although he had the technical knowledge to practice healing, he lacked the wisdom to turn the teachings into reality. He needed the key to turn on and activate the power. Usui decided to seek the final piece of the jigsaw through meditation.

Taking leave from the monastery, Usui set off for the holy mountain of Kurama. When he reached the top, he picked up twenty-one pebbles and placed them in front of himself. He sat down and began his meditation. Each day he threw away one pebble. For twenty-one days he prayed, meditated, sang and read the Sutras.

On the last day as he prayed, he asked God to show him the light. Suddenly, a bright light appeared in the sky and came rapidly towards him, hitting him on his forehead. Usui was knocked unconscious, and whilst in this altered state he saw a vision of the same ancient symbols he had earlier found in the Sutras. This vision was the confirmation Dr. Usui needed.

When Usui regained full consciousness, he proceeded to return down the mountain. On his descent, he stubbed and cut his toe, instinctively he placed his hand on the toe and the bleeding and pain stopped. On arrival at a nearby village he stopped to eat and rest. He was able, despite having fasted for 21 days, to eat a healthy meal without any stomach pain. The girl who served Usui the meal was in great pain suffering from a toothache. Usui asked if he could place his hands on her swollen face, she agreed, and he was able to ease the swelling and the pain. Rested, Usui returned to the monastery. On Arrival he found his friend, the Abbot in bed suffering with severe arthritis. Once again Usui was able to alleviate the pain and suffering. Usui called this gift from God – Reiki, the Japanese word for Universal Life Force. These experiences became known as the four miracles.

The rest of Usui's life was spent healing, teaching and developing the Usui Shiki Ryoho method of healing. Tenno, the Emperor of Japan honored Usui's work by awarding him a doctorate. Usui trained over 2,000 students before his death at age 62 and attuned nineteen major students as Reiki Masters. Dr Chujiro Hayashi was chosen as the next Grand Master. Dr Usui was cremated, and his ashes placed in a Zen Monastery in Tokyo.

DR CHUJIRO HAYASHI

Dr Chujiro Hayashi was born in Japan and was a qualified physician and retired Marine commander. Upon the death of Dr Usui, Hayashi was responsible for training a further sixteen Reiki Masters and creating a set formula for Reiki training, with hand positions to work with during a session and a more formal attunement process. He set up a clinic near the Emperor's palace in Tokyo called Shina No Macha. Each day his students held healing sessions at the clinic or visited people in their homes if they were unable to travel.

Hayashi went on to write many reports on the systems he had developed to treat various ailments. Special diets were incorporated into his treatments to assist the healing process. Probably his greatest advancement for Reiki was to discover the importance of whole-body treatment and how the Universal Life Force would go wherever it was needed to heal.

MADAME HAWAYO TAKATA

The third Grand Master to be appointed was Madame Takata, who had her own unique journey to Reiki and is accredited as taking Reiki to the West. Born Hawayo Kawamuru on the Island of Hawaii on 24th December 1900, Hawayo was married at the age of seventeen to Saichi Takata. They had a happy marriage with two daughters, however tragically, her husband died at the young age of thirty-two. After thirteen years of marriage, Hawayo Takata was left to raise two small children on her own.

The stress and pressure of the situation took its toll on her health. Within five years of her husband's death she was diagnosed with nervous exhaustion. Her health deteriorated to the point where she required surgery for a diseased gall bladder. However, she was also suffering from respiratory problems that meant the use of an anesthetic during surgery could kill her.

This was an extremely depressing and trying time in her life. Unfortunately, there was more pain and suffering to come when her sister died. As her parents had returned to live in Tokyo, it was her traditional responsibility to bring the news to them in person.

After her arrival in Japan, she sought help at a hospital in Akasaka. It was discovered that she now had a tumor and appendicitis to add to her diseased gallbladder and respiratory problems. Her weight dropped dramatically, and her doctor advised her to have immediate surgery.

That night as she lay in bed, she heard a voice saying, "The surgery is not necessary." The next day as she was being prepared for surgery, she heard the voice again saying, "The surgery is not necessary, ask – ask." Takata asked the surgeon if there was another way she could be healed, and he told her of the Reiki clinic run by Dr. Hayashi. The surgeon had a sister who had been there herself and had recovered fully from an illness.

Madam Takata went to the clinic and received treatments regularly for four months and was completely healed. She decided that she also wanted to learn Reiki and set up her own practice in Hawaii and she was eventually able to persuade Dr. Hayashi to allow her to work and train at the clinic for twelve months. At the end of this time it was felt that she had earned the privilege of receiving the second degree in Reiki – the advanced Practitioners' level.

In the summer of 1937, Madam Takata returned to Hawaii and set up her own Reiki clinic. She spent her time healing and teaching Reiki. Dr Hayashi visited Madam Takata in February 1938 and invited her to become a Reiki Master. She was the first woman to be given this honor, and the first Reiki Master from outside of Japan. She became the third Grand Master upon the passing of Dr Hayashi.

Madam Takata went on to train a further twenty-two Reiki Masters before her death in December 1980. There were two Grand Masters installed to continue Takata's work. Phyllis Lei Furumoto, the granddaughter of Madam Takata and Dr Barbara Weber. This partnership was to run for only a year until for personal reasons they split up to continue the work separately. The Reiki Alliance was formed by Phyllis, while Dr Weber set up the A.I.R.A. (The American International Reiki Association). Since then the powerful techniques of Reiki has been passed onto many generations of students, to help mankind and the wider animal kingdom. Reiki is now widely practiced across the globe.

As Reiki is taught from Reiki Master to Reiki student, we have a way of mapping any student's journey with Reiki back to Mikao Usui – this chain of Reiki Masters is displayed as a Reiki lineage – essentially, a Reiki family tree.

THE FIVE PRINCIPLES OF REIKI

"Gratitude turns what we have into enough."
– Anonymous.

Dr Usui believed that Reiki Practitioners needed a set of principles and values to guide them as they practiced Reiki and help them develop spiritually on their Reiki journey. These five principles can be summarized as the following five core beliefs:

- Just for today, I will not get angry
- Just for today, I will not worry
- Just for today, I will be grateful
- Just for today, I will work hard
- Just for today, I will be kind to every living creature

This last principle is very important in the study and practice of Animal Reiki. We want to be compassionate towards all creatures big and small, within our own homes and farther afield. Certainly, many Reiki Practitioners like to use their skills to work with rescue animals and shelters, and also to send positive energy to animals in crisis situations worldwide as their homes are threatened by natural disasters and human activity. Even the smallest acts of kindness to the animals we interact with, can do powerful things.

HOW DO WE CONNECT TO REIKI?

"Reiki is the greatest secret in the science of energetic." -Madam Hawayo Takata

Whilst Reiki is already written in our DNA and anyone can harness this profound, inbuilt and intelligent energy for healing, we must activate or plug into our energy channeling abilities via an attunement or initiation ceremony. An attunement essentially 'tunes' an individual back into this connection and increases the flow of energy in the body. Without being attuned to the Universal Life Force you will only be using about 10-20% of its capacity for healing.

During the attunement, A Reiki Master uses ancient Reiki symbols (passed down from master to master) and mantras (holy words that activate and direct certain energies) to connect the student to the Universal Life Force, essentially 'switching on' and super-charging the flow of energy. From the moment you are attuned to Reiki, the Universal Life Force will begin to flow through your hands at the thought of healing, and you can begin channeling the healing energy to yourself and others as well as animals. You can be attuned in person during a Reiki workshop or distantly, where a Reiki Master will work through the ceremony at a distance – both methods work the same and have the same impact.

Dr Hayashi explained it best when he described Reiki as being like radio waves. We cannot see them, but we know they are everywhere around us. When we turn on a radio and tune into the radio waves, we can pick up a signal. That signal is turned into a radio program. Similarly, the Universal Life Force is everywhere, but when we are tuned into the energy by a Reiki Master, we can harness Reiki to heal ourselves and others and send this healing across distances. "The energy is everywhere; it travels through space without wires. Once you have been connected to the energy it flows automatically, forever. It is a universal and immeasurable energy and its power is unlimited."

There are three levels of Reiki to master and be attuned to: Level 1 opens the practitioner as a channel for hands on healing, Level 2 allows the Practitioner to send healing distantly and after completing Reiki Level 3 the students become a Reiki Master – where they can then perform attunements themselves as they teach other students.

Is it important to emphasize that Reiki is always channeled through the Practitioner from a higher source to the recipient – it travels through you, not from you. So, you can never deplete your own supplies when working with an animal and equally you don't need to worry about disease or negative energy flowing back to you during a treatment. You are a channel for Reiki and the animal will draw the energy it needs through you. In this process, you also receive a self-treatment as the Reiki energy flows through you to the animal.

WHY IS REIKI IDEAL FOR TREATING ANIMALS?

"The greatness of a nation can be judged by the way its animals are treated." - Mahatma Gandhi

There are a number of reasons why Reiki is a great option for animals. For starters, we know they are deserving of love! Let's look now at some of the other main reasons why this complementary therapy is so well-suited to animals!

Animals are energetically sensitive

Animals are very sensitive to energy and love, which makes them an ideal recipient for energy healing. In fact, because animals are so sensitive to energy, most only need a small amount of Reiki unless they are ill, injured or have experienced abuse and neglect. Some Reiki session with an animal will only last a few minutes, as the animal draws in the energy it needs and walks away.

Reiki is intelligent

Reiki energy knows where to go to provide healing on physical, emotional, mental and spiritual levels. It is so powerful and intuitive that it will provide the healing that is most appropriate and beneficial to the animal, without the need for any specific instructions. This is important for working with animals as they cannot always communicate their needs or of course verbalize their symptoms (even though we may have a rough idea of what's going on and have medical information about their health from a vet). When the right intension it set, the energy needed will flow automatically from the universe, through the Practitioner to the animal.

Reiki is natural, safe & non-invasive

Reiki energy is grounded in love and balance. This simple yet powerful energy channeling system is gentle and non-invasive, which is important for animal-lovers who want their pets to feel comfortable. The animal can be treated in an environment they are familiar with, and there is no need to restrain the animal or cause any distress – the animal is in total control.

With regular treatment, the animal will become more familiar with the subtle energetic frequencies of Reiki and the impacts of a treatment and may start to approach the Practitioner for healing on their own accord.

The animal is in control of the outcome

As you are activating the animal's own ability to heal themselves, you are there to simply help the animal get the energy they need. As such, you should never enter a Reiki treatment with expectations or preconceptions about the outcomes of a treatment as the results are not down to you and cannot be forced or influenced! We don't know where the energy needs to go – there may be underlying issues or a complex mixture of energy imbalances that all need work! And whilst you can set the intention to work on a specific problem or dedicate more time to a specific area of the body that the animal is having issues with, the animal will draw the energy it needs to heal in a way that promotes the greatest and highest good for them. This is a pretty reassuring feature of Reiki, especially when you first start practicing - you don't need to overthink it, overanalyze, over-prepare or question yourself - the energy will go where it needs to!

Reiki can help the animal and the owner!

When a Reiki Practitioner channels Reiki to an animal, they too are surrounded by the healing power and love of Reiki. As they give a treatment the Reiki energy flows through them providing healing to both the Practitioner and the animal. It is a beautiful gift and a way to give back to the animals in our lives. Because it is so easy to learn, any pet owner or animal lover can master the basics and begin to work with their pets!

HOW DOES REIKI WORK?

"Reiki is Love, Love is wholeness, wholeness is balance, balance is wellbeing, wellbeing is freedom from disease." Dr Mikao Usui

Have you ever felt like someone is looking at you and then looked up to see someone staring? Or felt someone standing close by even though you weren't touching? Have you walked into a situation and felt instantly uncomfortable? These are examples of when we naturally become aware of the subtle energies of our body and our environment.

Take a moment to test this energy.

Put your hand in front of your body, with your palms facing each other. Move your hands closer together but do not let them touch. Then move your hands away. Move your hands back and forth slowly. What can you notice as you move your hands closer together? Do you notice any sensations? Do you feel any heat? That's energy!

But what is energy?

By definition, energy is the 'ability to do work' which essentially means energy is how things change and move. Energy is everywhere around us and exists in many different forms – including heat, light and electrical energy.

Thermodynamics is the study of energy. The First Law of Thermodynamics states that the total amount of energy in a Universe remains constant, it cannot be created or destroyed, it simply changes from one form to another.

The human body is an energy transformation machine – we convert the chemical energy stored in the food we eat into the mechanical energy that moves our muscles, the thermal energy that keeps our body temperature constant, and the electrical energy that sends nerve impulses in our nervous system.

When we look at life at sub-atomic level – again we see energy.

Each of our cells is made up of tiny atoms which are made of even smaller units – protons, neutrons and electrons. These building blocks emit waves of electrical energy that vibrate at their own speed or frequency.

All matter is made up of energy. Every being in the universe is therefore connected at this energetic level. Eastern traditions denote this life-giving energy as Ki – the Universal Life Force. This energy is in a constantly state of movement, nothing is static but different objects will move at different speeds. It is the differences between these unique energy frequencies that makes different objects appear as separate entities– humans, animals, plants etc. This is the basis of The Law of Vibration.

Just as our physical bodies (blood, bones, muscles etc.) have their own energetic properties, our thoughts, emotional and spiritual intuition are vibrating at their own frequencies, creating an energy field that surrounds the human body. This is the same for animals and all living things.

This energy field consists of multiple, interconnected layers of energy outside the physical body, each with their own vibrational energy. These interacting energy layers are collectively known as an aura (pronounced 'Oar-Ruh').

Aura is a Latin word which means 'light' or 'glow of light' which reflects the experience that many report when they see the aura – it is described as an all-encompassing hazy bubble of colorful and glowing light which surrounds the whole physical body. The aura acts at the connection from the physical body to the energy in the universe.

The aura is widely reported as consisting of seven layers in both humans and animals – also known as the seven auric layers. Because the energy layers in the aura vibrate at higher speeds than the energy within the body, they do not appear as solid entities and are invisible to most – although subtle energy can be detected with the aid of a special photography technique known as Kirlian photography. The frequency of energy vibration increases as you move away from the physical body so that each layer vibrates at a different speed and produces a different color of light. Experienced Reiki Masters can see and feel its colors.

Overall, these colors within the aura are in a constant state of change – a shifting rainbow of swirling light which will flux with life's challenges and events. Essentially, the aura is colored by health or illness, love and hate or anger, personal strength or weakness, happiness or sorrow, and the extent of our spiritual journey in this life.

Together, these layers generally take on an egg-like shape around the physical body. When people say they can feel or sense someone's energy in their proximity, just as we tested with our palms a moment ago, they are sensing the interactions of the subtle auric fields. It is important to note, that whilst you may begin to see the auric energies the more you work with Reiki, you don't need to see or feel anything to be able to work with Reiki on animals!

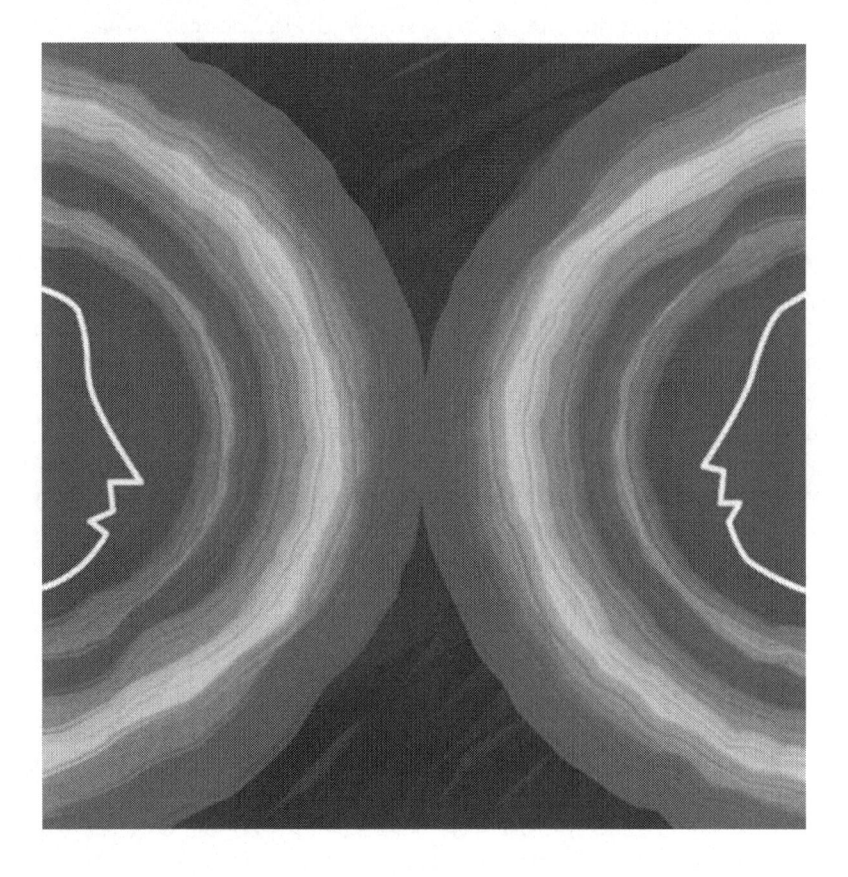

AURAS IN ANIMALS

*"If you want to find the secrets of the universe,
think in terms of energy, frequency and vibration."*
- Nikola Tesla

Animals are physical, emotional and spiritual beings just like humans, and the aura of an animal is a real-time expression of their physical, emotional and spiritual self.

The main difference between the aura of humans and other animals is the extension of certain layers. Many experienced Animal Reiki Masters note that the emotional body in animals extends far wider than humans, whilst the mental layers of the aura are narrower given that animals do not use or develop the same complex mental processes and capacities as humans do.

Animals experience fear, grief, panic, love, anger, care, play, lust and other emotions just like humans, and search for purpose and meaning just like humans. Animals are constantly exploring where they belong and their connection to other living things and the divine on a spiritual level. The spiritual layers of their aura are well developed as a result.

As animals are more receptive to energy than humans, they're ability to see and sense aura is enhanced. It is how they interact and recognize other animals and their human companions. They read our energy as soon as they meet us.

As you start to practice animal Reiki you may begin to experience auras. Some people see auras, others sense or feel them. Let's work through two exercises you can practice to start to develop your ability to feel or sense an animal's aura. It's best to practice first with your own pet, or a small domestic animal you know well and is comfortable around you.

Feeling an animal's Aura

1. Stand or sit next to the animal you are working on – again making sure this is an animal you are comfortable with and know.
2. Take a few deep breaths. Clear your mind of any thoughts of preconceptions. Become aware of your breathing to center you mind in the current moment.
3. When you are relaxed and centered, squint your eyes slightly so you can follow your hands.
4. Hold your hands about 8 inches away from the animal's skin/fur.
5. Slowly allow your hands to drop closer towards the animal. As you do so be alert to any feelings or sensation in your hands. Do you sense a compelling pull or any resistance?
6. When you feel like you have detected the edge of the aura, allow your hands to float at this level along the animal's back. Do you notice that your hands drop suddenly closer to the animal at any point? Do you notice any difference in the energy? This may be a reflection of a weakened aura.
7. Remember this is subtle energy we are dealing with, so you may need to practice this over time before you notice or feel anything. Practice this exercise a few times and make notes of what you experience as you strengthen your abilities.

Sensing an animal's aura

1. Find a safe, quiet space, making sure the animal you are going to be working on is close by.
2. Close your eyes and take several calming breaths.
3. Clear your mind of any thoughts of preconceptions. Become aware of your breathing to center your mind in the current moment.

4. Turn your attention now to the energy surrounding the animal near you.
5. Is there a bright strong energy surrounding the animal or is the energy weak and imbalanced? Is the energy calm or agitated? Do you notice any colors?
6. Practice this exercise and make a note of what you observe. Do not worry if you don't feel that you can sense the energy at first. With practice, a calm mind and centered energy, you will begin to become more aware of the subtle energy systems. Remember that you don't need to see an aura to work with Reiki - so don't be disappointed if you can't see them, everyone is different.

THE ENERGY CENTERS IN ANIMALS

"There is no fundamental difference between man and animals in their ability to feel pleasure and pain, happiness, and misery." - Charles Darwin

Each layer of the aura is connected to the physical body via an energy point or center known as a Chakra (pronounced 'Chuhk-Ruh'). These energy centers regulate the flow of energy between the body and the mental, emotional and spiritual energies stored in the aura. So, they are essentially the gateways to our energy systems.

Chakra is actually a Sanskrit word that translates as 'wheel' or 'circle.' You may have seen drawings and illustrations of the chakras as swirling energy vortices spiraling outwards into the aura. As they spin, they emit different frequencies of light which radiate as different colors that can be seen by some Reiki Masters.

When the chakras are spinning correctly throughout our bodies, energy flows through like an unimpeded river, bringing health and wellbeing to every area of our existence. If one of the wheels becomes damaged or stops completely, then the flow is broken and may stagnate – these blockages can manifest as disease and illness across the whole system, contaminating the energy supply. This is why it is important that the chakras are balanced.

Like humans, animals have seven major chakras: the Crown chakra, Third Eye Chakra, Throat Chakra, Heart Chakra, Solar Plexus Chakra, the Sacral and the Root Chakra. Each of these chakras have different locations in the body feeding energy to the mind, body and spirit, influencing specific body systems, emotions and behaviors. Just like in humans, two of the chakras (the Crown and Third Eye Chakra) are located in the head. The other five are found as you move down the body (as shown below). They are the same for all animals, large and small.

Crown Chakra
Top of the head

Third Eye Chakra
Middle of the forehead

Solar Plexus Chakra
Middle of the back

Sacral Chakra
Lower belly

Throat Chakra
In the throat

Heart Chakra
Centre of the chest

Root Chakra
Base of the spine

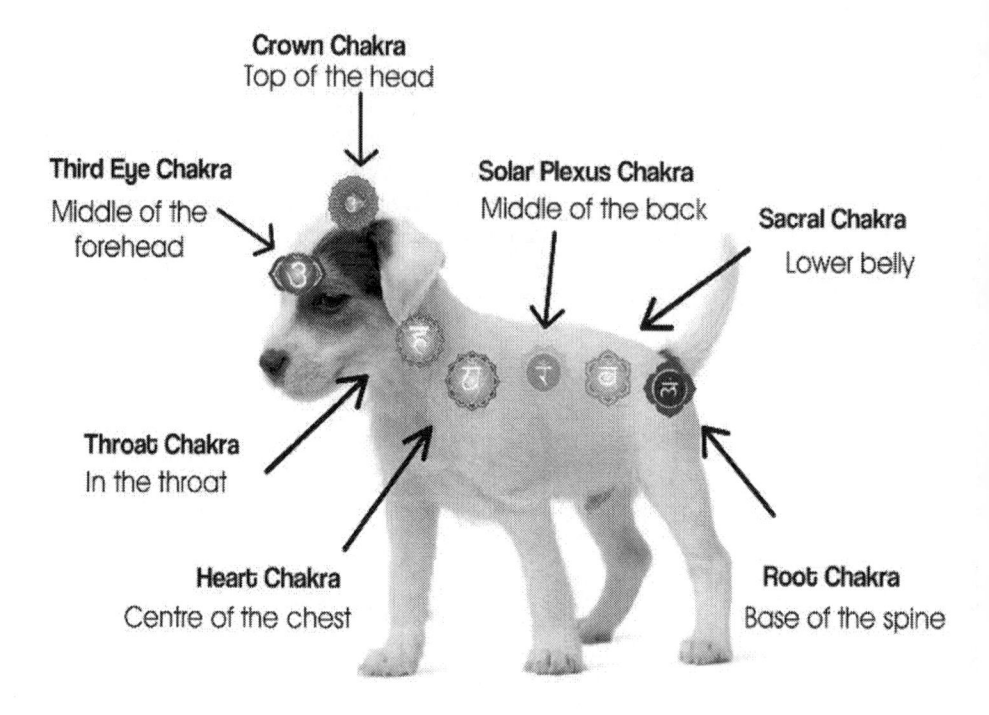

When one or more of the chakra energy centers is not working correctly, the body may become sick or in pain as the flow of life-force energy is unbalanced. These imbalances may cause issues with the body systems, emotions and behaviors that the chakra control, and these issues can give us clues to the parts of the energy system that need some Reiki energy.

A full Reiki treatment reopens the chakras and gets them spinning correctly, re-balancing the flow of Universal Life Force around the body to maintain health and provide healing on all levels. We can channel energy to the chakra and set the intention to bring each chakra into optimum balance if it is dull, blocked, overactive or inactive.

Which Energy Centers Need Reiki?

Chakra	Organs and Systems	Signs of Imbalance
Base Chakra	Excretory systems and spine	Fearful, flight reaction, lack of trust, insecurity, detachment, restless, lazy, greedy, bone disorders, conditions of the feet and legs, slowing down.
Sacral Chakra	Reproductive system	Weakness, low confidence, lower back pain, obsessed with sexual needs, fertility issues, boundaries issues, difficulty differentiating work/training with play, sterility, sexual dysfunction.
Solar Plexus Chakra	Digestive system	Digestive issues, eating problems, diabetes, aggressiveness, overly dominant or submissive, withdrawn, avoids everyone, colic, ulcers.
Heart Chakra	Circulatory system	Grief, sadness, nervous around other animals/human, inability to bond, reclusive, possessive/jealous. Blood disorders, auto-immune diseases, lung conditions.
Throat Chakra	Lungs, vocal apparatus	Excessively noisy or lack of vocalization, does not response to training or commands, thyroid issues, teething, gum problems or tooth decay, biting.
Third Eye Chakra	Lower brain, nervous system, ears, nose, eyes	Poor vision, deafness, doesn't listen, confusion, overreaction to sounds, anxious, distracted, distant, intolerance or stubbornness. Hormonal imbalances. Skin allergies, hair loss.
Crown Chakra	Upper brain	Poor vision, despression, neediness, seperation anxiety, shy, lonely, seizures, learning difficulties, senility.

MINOR AND BUD CHAKRAS IN ANIMALS

In addition to the seven major chakras, there are several smaller energy points in the animal body, known as the Minor Chakras and Bud Chakras, which deal with the sensory systems of the animal. Animals rely on their senses to understand and respond to their environment and are continually absorbing sensory information.

There are 21 minor chakras that can be found throughout the body and act to assist the major chakras in their functions. The minor chakras work specifically on the sensory systems. The most significant minor chakras are found at the tail, tip of the nose and ears.

Animals also have 6 bud chakras – four in the footpads/hooves of the animal, and two at the base of the ear openings. These bud chakras are sensory receptors which respond to very subtle changes in the environment – picking up on small vibrational changes. This is why animals seem to be able to anticipate changes in weather well before humans for example.

Although the minor and bud chakras are smaller in size than the major chakras they are just as essential to the overall health of the animal. People that are able to see chakras have described the minor and bud chakras appearing as bright rings of shimmering light with white and blue sparks. We treat the minor and bud chakras by channeling Reiki to the major chakra points.

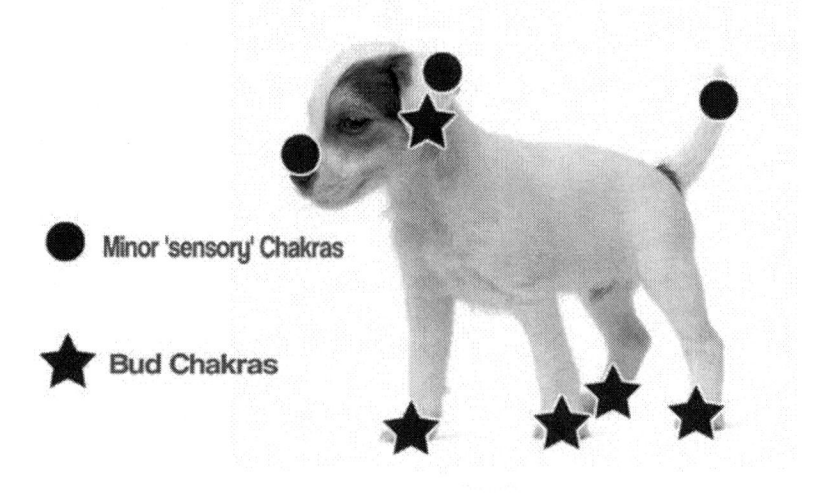

● Minor 'sensory' Chakras

★ Bud Chakras

WHAT HAPPENS DURING AN ANIMAL REIKI SESSION?

"You can always tell about somebody by the way they put their hands on an animal." - Betty White

Although every session will vary based on the animal and their energy needs – in essence, every session involves four stages:

1. Connect with the Universe Life Force, opening yourself up as a channel for Reiki.
2. Infuse the energy with your healing intention.
3. Channel the Universal Life Force to the animal – work to specific charkas or where you feel you are guided to work. Either way Reiki will go where is needs to! And you will start sharing energy the moment you place your hands on an animal's body.

4. When the animal has drawn the energy it needs, it's time to let go, close down and end the session. The animal may show a number of distinct reactions which you can use to guide your session and also know when to finish.

An animal will normally need four full treatments on four consecutive days to boost the flow of Reiki energy. This will stimulate the body's immune system and natural healing abilities. The seven chakras are activated starting with the Root and ending with the Crown. This is the beginning of a cleansing detoxifying cycle as the whole energy system is rebalanced and reconnected to the healing Universal Life Force. Reiki energy goes to work to release emotional or physical barriers, blocks or baggage stored in the body throughout the lifetime of the animal. Reiki's wisdom will do the rest! Remember, a little bit of Reiki is always better than none!

When it's time to start channeling Reiki, there are several treatment methods a Reiki Practitioner can work with during an animal Reiki treatment: hands-on Reiki, Beaming Reiki and Distant Reiki. In all methods of Reiki healing, your hands will act as the channel for Reiki to flow to the animal, with energy flowing as soon as you set your intention and connect to the Universal Life Force.

HANDS-ON REIKI

Those beautiful moments we share with our pets when they come and sit, stand or lay by our side, provide the perfect opportunity to work with hands-on Reiki, as you pet and lovingly comfort the animal. Indeed, hands-on Reiki – where you perform Reiki with your hands directly on the animal or hovering slightly above – is ideal for pets and animals that you know well. They are comfortable with your touch and energy presence and you are able to connect with them at the most peaceful times in their day, as you are already familiar with their habits and behaviors. You can also more easily read and respond to their verbal and non-verbal cues, for example, they may move towards your hands and sit under them, push their body directly into your hands, or remain very still and relaxed close to you. You may experience an instant and strong energy flow through your hands, signaling that they would appreciate some Reiki energy.

Hands-on Reiki should never be used for wild, aggressive or dangerous animals, or in any situation where the animal is confused, nervous, sick, hurt or in pain, or if your safety may be jeopardized by approaching the animal. As a rule, you should always start an animal Reiki session at a distance with an animal you don't know well and never approach or touch them unless they have given you the permission to do so, you have spoken to the animal's owner, and you feel completely comfortable and safe.

Of course, even with our own animal companions we still have to be very cautious of their animal instincts and reactions – you wouldn't, for example, stand within kicking distance of a horse as you move around the back of the animal. And the same goes for other animal guardians – still remain cautious even if the owner is confident that the animal is safe to work with. If in doubt, proceed with Reiki at a safe distance. In fact, most animals actually prefer their first few interactions with Reiki to be at least from a short distance and will move in and out of your proximity throughout the treatment so you can use a combination of both hands-on and distant Reiki.

When hands-on Reiki is appropriate, you can work through a series of hand positions during a session just like you would do with a human hands-on Reiki treatment. There isn't a formal set of hand positions for animals, but we can use a set of positions that are aligned to an animal's major and minor chakra points as a way of working on the whole energy system. Whilst some people do prefer to work through all the chakras in full, it is important to note that hand positions are only a guide, you can work from one area of the animal's body for the whole session or just focus in on a particular one or two chakras if you prefer. Remember Reiki energy will always go where it is needed.

If you are going to be touching the animal, make sure you do so very softly and that your hands are warm. The hands should be cupped slightly with fingers together to concentrate the flow of energy and stop energy dissipating through your fingers. As you work on a chakra, you can visualize opening up this energy center just as you would open a door, letting pure white energy flow through into the chakra and wash over the animal.

BEAMING REIKI

There will be times when you can't directly touch an animal and times when the animal doesn't want to be touched or even have your hands very close to their body. They may be in pain, anxious, very large or small. We must also be aware that when treating some common pets like fish or insects you may not be able to get close to the animal because they are in a tank or enclosure. Other animals may be in a kennel, stall or a cage.

In cases like these we can practice 'beaming' Reiki a short distance, where you can visualize a beam of Reiki energy streaming from your hands to the whole animal or a specific area of the body for healing. With beaming, the animal is usually in the same room or only a short distance away.

There are a number of ways that beaming Reiki can come in handy. Beaming is a common way to start a Reiki session at a distance, to allow the animal to feel more relaxed as it gets used to the Reiki energy. You can ask the animal to step into the beam when it is ready. For small animals you can use beaming to surround the animal in a bubble of healing energy. You can also perform a full body treatment by beaming Reiki to each of the animal's chakra points.

When you are carrying out a hands-on session it is common to switch between the traditional hands-on method and beaming as the animal moves around the treatment space, so it's good to practice both methods when you are starting out.

Another safe way to indirectly treat animals is by working on their food and drink. Whilst this is a slightly weaker form of Reiki treatment, taking the time to beam Reiki to the animal's water source and their meals is one way of increasing their contact with the Universal Life Force. You can also channel Reiki to bath water when washing and grooming your pets as well as beaming Reiki to their living spaces.

DISTANT REIKI

When you progress to Reiki Level 2 you will learn about Distant Reiki – this is where you can use visualization techniques and the ancient Reiki symbols to send Reiki over distances, and even across time. We won't touch too much on this advanced technique in this beginner's guide, but it is important to be aware of it. Distant Reiki is just as effective as hands-on healing and the amazing thing about distant Reiki is that it allows us to work with animals all over the world. We can send healing across time to stressful situations to provide relaxation to pets and animals.

We believe all sessions should begin at a distance unless you a very familiar with the animal yourself. Other situations where distant Reiki is essential include: working with wild or aggressive animals, if you are frightened or uncomfortable with an animal, if the animal is very stressed, anxious or mistrusting of humans due to neglect or abuse, if the animal is very ill and working near the animal will cause discomfort or injury and if the animal cannot be touched (e.g. marine life, pregnant animals).

There may be occasions when an animal will move back and forth from your hands during a session. This is totally normal behavior and you shouldn't be discouraged. If the animal moves away, you can always continue the session by beaming Reiki energy from a short distance or by sending Reiki distantly from further away.

Indeed, most practitioners work with a combination of the above techniques which they adapt and use to respond to the needs of the individual animal and protect their own safety.

IMPORTANT CONSIDERATIONS WHEN TREATING AN ANIMAL WITH REIKI

"Animals are the bridge between us and the beauty of all that is natural." —— Trisha McCagh

When getting ready to work with an animal, there are a few really important considerations to be aware of. All Animal Reiki Practitioners should respect these considerations when treating an animal including their own pets. We have discussed some of these key factors already in earlier sections, but let's take a moment to review everything here in one place!

SAFETY FIRST, ALWAYS

Whilst animals are amazing creatures capable of great love, they can also be very unpredictable, and it is paramount to consider your own safety when working with any animal. As we have mentioned, not all animals are comfortable being touched or around humans and we have to respect this to make sure we are safe, and of course they are happy. Its best to always start the session at a distance to assess the animal's temperament and allow them to sense and respond to the Reiki energy. For wild, scared or dangerous animals, always begin with a barrier between you and the animal - a fence, a cage, a gate etc.

Animals will quickly show you if they are uncomfortable - they may run away or hide, or become verbally distressed (for example barking, growling, hissing etc.) or lash out with scratches, kicks and bites. You must respect when an animal does not want to be touched or even near you.

During a Reiki session, if the animal becomes aggressive or restless, it is best to pause the session immediately and move a safe distance away. Likewise, if at any time you feel unsafe or notice a change in the animal's mood or energy it is always best to stop. Never force an animal into a treatment – you can always try again another day or give the animal the choice to receive the energy distantly now or in the future when they are more at ease with receiving help.

Before you start practicing Reiki as a professional on animal clients, you will need to check the laws and regulations for animal Reiki in your country/state and always work within these guidelines to make sure you are protected and your clients are too.

ASK FOR PERMISSION FROM THE OWNER

If the animal is not your own pet, then you need to ask the owner for permission to work with Reiki on their animal. If the owner is new to Reiki, it's important to explain how Reiki can help and benefit their animal, and what's involved in a standard animal Reiki treatment. You should make them aware that you are purely acting as a conduit for Reiki energy and not healing the animal – making sure they understand that you are not in control of the outcomes of the treatment– the animal takes the energy it needs and uses it for optimum relaxation, health and wellbeing. This means the treatment may end unexpectedly – this is beyond the practitioner's control. It is important they understand that several sessions may be needed to allow the animal to achieve the results that work best for them.

Ultimately it is important to reassure the owner that Reiki can do no harm and you are only there to help the animal. That said, they are still in control of the pet's care and should always maintain responsibility for the animal's health and wellbeing. Whilst Reiki will not affect or hinder any other treatments an animal is receiving from a veterinary professional, the owner should always consult their vet before any Reiki sessions and report any changes or health issues to the vet.

Some owners will let you know if the animal has any existing illnesses, injuries, behavioral problems or medical diagnoses that they have received from the vet. This is great information as it can help you focus on a certain area or chakra during a Reiki session. They may also pass on advice from the vet about areas of the animal's body that may be very sensitive to touch, such as a bandaged broken bone. Equally, be aware that some owners will prefer not to share specific information about a diagnosis from a vet with you. This is fine too - Reiki energy will always flow to where it is most needed anyway.

It is important to state here, that you should never claim that you can 'cure' or 'fix' an animal in any way. Nor should you offer medical advice or diagnosis. Remember, you are not in control of the outcomes and you aren't there to prove that Reiki works – just focus on helping the animal get the energy it needs.

Although Reiki will never do any harm to a pet or animal, we do live in a world where we need to protect ourselves as professionals. As well as having adequate professional practitioner insurance, it is also a good idea to use a waiver form to clarify and confirm the responsibilities of the pet owner ahead of a session.

ASK THE PERMISSION OF THE ANIMAL

Now this may sound a bit strange, but it is a really important part of animal Reiki. The animal is active part of the healing process and just as you would ask a human for their permission to begin a Reiki treatment, it's important to give the animal the same control over the session. Some people like to verbally let the animal know what they are about to do asking for permission to continue. There will be some animals that instinctively recognize your healing energy and will approach you to receive it. If the animal gives signs that they are comfortable with you remaining with them (they relax, remain very still, sit or lay down, swim closer to you, fall asleep or stay nearby), then you can continue.

Other people work more intuitively in their mind's eye, telepathically asking the animal for their permission to proceed. The important thing, whatever method you use, is to reassure the animal that they can draw as much or as little energy through you as they see fit. There is no pressure to accept the energy, and they can move away or hide and end the session at any point. They have free will and we are not here to force animals to do something they don't want to do. If the animal seems unsure, you can always begin the session and monitor how they respond as the session goes on. Animals will approach you and make it clear they are comfortable if they want to receive Reiki.

In cases where it's not possible to get permission, for example if the animal is asleep or unconscious in an emergency situation, when you infuse the Reiki energy with your healing intention, just make sure that you state that the Reiki energy should only go where it is needed. It the animal does not want to receive it; it should flow somewhere where it is needed more.

WHERE SHOULD YOU CONDUCT A REIKI SESSION WITH AN ANIMAL?

Ideally you want the treatment space for an animal Reiki session to be quiet, so you should take a moment to remove distractions, this could include switching your mobile phone off or turning off on a noisy TV set. If there are any other people home at the time let them know that you are about to start a session, to ensure they will not disturb you by accident. Some people choose to play some calming music softly in the background to relax the animal, but this may be too much for some animals and you should always consider their comfort.

It is important to perform Reiki in an environment where the animal can roam freely and not feel constricted. Giving an animal the freedom to move, experience and respond to Reiki as they see fit should always be the main objective.

Wherever you set up the treatment space, make sure to find a comfortable position that you can keep throughout the treatment, whether that's sitting on the floor, in a chair or standing if you prefer. When you are working with animals outside it may be useful to have a foldable chair or stool handy.

During the Reiki session, animals may become dehydrated due to all of the energy flowing through their bodies. It is a good idea to have water available to the animal throughout the treatment and directly afterwards. You should also stay hydrated for the same reason.

THE ENERGY DETOX

Another thing you should be aware of in advance of an animal Reiki session is energy detoxing. As Reiki works to rebalance the animal's energy system, the body works to clear any toxins that inhibit the energy. Just like a dietary detox, cleansing an animal's energy system may result in symptoms of physical detoxification such as a running nose, cough or diarrhea. We can see the same symptoms in humans after a Reiki session. These symptoms will soon pass – but it's important to be aware of them.

To help the detoxing process along, there are some things the animal's owner can do. The most important thing is providing love and support for the animal. Let the animal rest when needed following a session but do make sure they have the opportunity to get exercise, fresh air and mental stimulation should their condition permit it. Reducing their exposure to unnatural products such as shampoos, perfumes or flea treatments can be beneficial if they are not medically prescribed. Diet is really imperative too – as well as avoiding feeding the animal your own leftovers or heavily processed foods, it is important to provide fresh food and water every day, with species appropriate nutrients. Replace dry kibble food with wet or fresh snacks if appropriate. But speak to your vet to get the best information for your animal. Obviously if a vet has set a medically prescribed diet you wouldn't want change this, and you would never stop any medications or treatments, diet or routines, without consulting your vet.

HOW LONG DOES AN ANIMAL REIKI SESSION LAST?

As animals are very sensitive to Reiki, some sessions may be very short. In fact, we find that animals often like shorter treatments more often. Usually a Reiki practitioner will set aside about an hour for the treatment with the owner or caregivers, with the expectation that they may require more or less time depending on the animal and their needs. On the first session with the animal, you would allocate slightly more time to the session to speak with the owner and find a suitable space, making sure you also allow some time to talk with the owner afterwards.

You may wonder what time of day is best for an animal Reiki session. Whilst you can obviously practice Reiki at any time, ideally you would choose a time when the animal is most relaxed and calm, for example after they have gone for a long walk or had a meal. Within the time slot that you have agreed it's best to wait until the animal is most relaxed and calm, where possible, before starting the treatment.

Remember that Reiki may be too much for very unwell animals – if this is the case or they seem uncomfortable in any way, you should not proceed with a Reiki session.

WORKING WHEN EMOTIONS RUN HIGH

There may be cases where you are working with very sick, abused or neglected animals. These situations can be very distressing - seeing an animal in pain or very upset can be hard to bear. Of course, you should never try to touch an animal that is very troubled, anxious, confused or sick. If you feel the animal is comfortable receiving Reiki from a short distance, and have spoken to the owner for their permission, it's vital that you enter the session with loving energy and focus on the love and healing we can channel to the animal – feelings of grief or pity send the wrong emotional energy signals to the animal. Just take a step back from the situation if it becomes too emotional charged and send healing to yourself until you feel composed enough to continue. We cannot change the animal's past, but we can positively contribute to their current situation and accepting this is key to vibrating hopeful healing energy.

OTHER PRACTICAL CONSIDERATIONS

Let's run through some other practical considerations that you might like to consider before you start a Reiki session.

- We recommended wearing loose fitting closing so that you are comfortable throughout the session and Reiki is able to flow freely through you.
- When working with animals avoid wearing anything that may distract the animal such as dangling fabrics or straps, for example a pussy bow shirt or a tie may prove to be the ultimate distraction for a curious feline!
- The healing energy of Reiki can travel through all materials including metals. However, we like to remove jewelry such as rings, necklaces and watches before starting a Reiki session as the metals in these can come into contact with and attract negative energy.
- It's best to smell clean and fresh when working with an animal. Many animals have a heightened sense of smell so we would advise to avoid wearing strong perfumes or aftershaves, you don't want the animal to be distracted or uncomfortable.
- It's a good idea to eat healthy food that won't leave you sluggish before a Reiki session. Make sure you don't start a session on an empty stomach, feeling hungry, as this will be distracting for you.
- Hydration is also really important. A Reiki session can leave you feeling dehydrated so it's a good idea to drink plenty of water to feel alert. Alcohol can dissipate energy so it's best to avoid it twenty-four hours before a session.
- You are acting as a channel for pure and loving Reiki energy and you want to feel fresh and well-rested so make sure you get a good night's sleep the day before a session.

HOW TO START AN ANIMAL REIKI SESSION

"The intention is key to Reiki." - Garry Malone

As you now know, unless you are working with your own pet or a pet you know well that is comfortable with you working close to them, you should always start a treatment from a distance. Begin by approaching the animal very slowly, staying ten feet away from the animal to introduce yourself and open up the channel to Reiki. Place your palms out in front of you but lowered so as not to seem threatening and meditate on your intentions to heal the animal, so they can begin to familiarize themselves with this new Reiki energy from a comfortable distance. It's advisable not to stare at the animal, as too much eye contact can intimidate an animal or appear threatening.

You want the animal to approach you throughout the treatment rather than approaching them. When you do begin the treatment, always allow the animal to move freely around the treatment space. As they become more relaxed and trusting they may end up close to your hands but be aware it may take some time for them to settle into the treatment and appreciate the energy they are receiving. They may rub against your hands, sniff your hands or nudge your hands with their head – all signs they are inviting you to channel Reiki.

If you are working on your own pet, for example a dog that's used to sitting snuggled on your lap, you can take advantage of these relaxed and calm moments and start a Reiki session.

MAKING SURE YOU ARE CALM AND CENTERED

It is very important to assess your own emotional, mental and spiritual state before starting a Reiki session with an animal because animals can easily sense and respond to our energies. If you are particularly worried that day or nervous, the animal may pick up on this. They may respond by keeping a distance or if they are unsure of your intentions and feel threatened, things could turn aggressive if they go on the defensive to try to protect themselves. A scared or defensive animal is going to be less likely to accept Reiki energy, so it's really important we check our energy before we start a Reiki session.

The key is to arrive calm, centered and confident. By following all the necessary safety steps outlined previously you can give yourself peace of mind and focus on the session ahead. Make sure you practice working through a full session with your own pets or the pets of close friends and family before you start treating other animals, as you will develop your confidence through practice.

Some Reiki Masters like to take a moment ahead of a session to center themselves. There are a number of ways that you can do this, including a quick Reiki self-treatment, a meditation, deep breathing or even enjoying a cool glass of water or your favorite tea.

We have outlined two simple meditation techniques you can use to center yourself before a Reiki session: the Gassho meditation and the Chakra Meditation.

Gassho Meditation

In the Gassho meditation, you use the Gassho prayer position. Gassho is a Japanese term that translates literally as "two hands coming together." It is the most fundamental ritual hand gesture or 'mudra' in Reiki. Mudras are specific and symbolic hand gestures used during meditation to draw your focus inward and channel your body's energy flow. Over a hundred mudras have been developed, but the Gassho is the most commonly used mudra in the practice of Buddhism. The Gassho hand position is formed by placing the palms together, in the 'prayer' or 'praying hands' position (with the palms touching and your fingertips pointing to the sky). You can hold your hands in front of your chest, over your lips and nose or in front of your forehead. Concentrate on the place where your two middle fingers touch to focus the mind and center yourself in that moment.

Chakra Meditation

Another meditation technique that can be used to open yourself up to the flow of Reiki energy ahead of an animal treatment is a simple chakra mediation. As the seven chakras in the body are all interconnected, it is better to meditate on all seven to open up the energy centers and bring them into balance so you can act as a powerful channel for Reiki.

1. Sit down in a quiet and comfortable space. Rest your hands naturally on your knees.
2. Take a few deep breaths to center your body and relieve tension, breathing naturally. Clear your mind, letting go of thoughts, distractions and preconceptions.
3. Close your eyes and focus your attention on your Root Chakra – the energy center that is found at the base of the spine. Visualize a connection from your body to earth below. You may want to place your hands in front of the chakra as you do so. Focus on the color red – the color associated with this chakra– and visualize energy flowing in and through the chakra just like a swirling galaxy or whirlpool – meditate on that for a few minutes until the color is bright and vibrant.
4. Repeat this process for each chakra as you move up to the top of the body. We will run through the chakras now.
5. Shift your focus to your Sacral Chakra and its creative energy – this is found just below the navel and its associated color is orange. Focus on the color orange and meditate on that for a few minutes.
6. Next, move to your Solar Plexus Chakra in the stomach area and focus on the color yellow.
7. Move up to your Heart Chakra, found in the center of the chest, focusing on the color green.
8. Shift your focus to the Throat Chakra, located in the base of the throat. Focus on the color bright blue.
9. Now shift your focus to the Third Eye Chakra which is found in the forehead between the eyes, focusing on the color indigo.
10. Next shift your focus to the Crown Chakra found at the top of the head. Focus on the color violet.
11. Visualize the energy flowing through and out of the Crown Chakra to immerse your body in a bright light. Feel its warmth and love.

12. Finally visualize the energy flowing freely from the Root to the Crown Chakra and out to surround the body. Repeat this step until you feel the energy flowing through your chakras and around your body.
13. When you reach this state, take a deep breath and open your eyes.

It's a good idea to practice daily meditation to develop a technique that works best for you. The more you practice, the easier you will find it to move into that calm state to begin a Reiki session. There are many other meditation techniques that you can explore and practice to find one that works for you!

CONNECT TO REIKI

When you are calm and centered you can begin to open yourself up to Reiki. Different Reiki Masters like to connect to Reiki in different ways, but here are some helpful steps that you can use to sense the energy flowing.

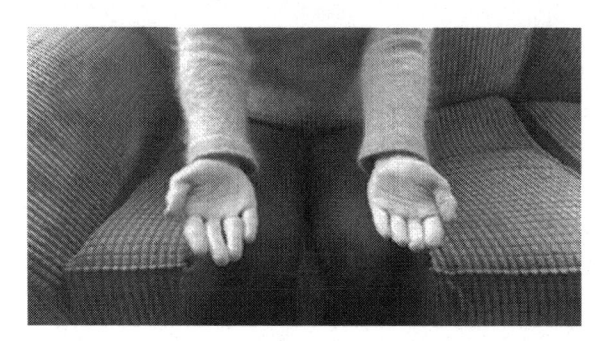

1. Place your palms hands up on your thighs, keeping your fingers together so your hands are slightly cupped.
2. Visualize a bright white light streaming down into your body through your Crown chakra on the top of your head.
3. Feel this warming, loving, pure white light fill your whole body.
4. Now visualize this glorious white light energy emitting from your palms and mediate on this energy.
5. Move you palms closer together but without touching as if you are catching a ball of energy. Play with this ball of energy for a moment – stretch and compress the energy. Experience the sensation – it may feel

warm or tingle slightly. You may wish to rub your hands together intermittently whilst playing with this energy.
6. Remember the goal isn't to feel anything specifically, but to be open to whatever happens. Reiki works even if you don't feel anything!
7. Go back to the rest position with your palms on your thighs – you are now ready to set the intention for the session.

SET THE INTENTION

With Reiki, intention is everything! When we talk about intention, we mean the positive end result or outcome we are hoping for when we open ourselves up as a channel for Reiki. Whilst we can never assume that we know what's best for the animal, we can commit to one clear goal: being a channel for Reiki energy to allow the animal to draw the energy it needs to heal where it's needed most.

Reciting an invocation (short prayer) in your mind or out loud at the beginning of every session helps to set this pure intention. Whilst this is not required to 'switch on Reiki,' we find that it helps us to center ourselves and stay grounded.

The invocation is personal to you and your own beliefs and an opportunity to ask that you become a channel for Reiki healing. We will go through our personal invocation now that you can use wholly or as a guideline for developing your own invocation.

Our Invocation

"I call upon Reiki – the Universal Life Force, all the Angelic beings who have worked with Reiki in the past especially Dr. Usui, Dr. Hayashi, Madam Takata, my guides and all the Reiki Masters past, present and future to draw near and take part in this healing session.

I ask that the power and wisdom of Reiki permits me to become a channel for Reiki's unconditional love and healing, on behalf of_____ (insert animal's name*) may Reiki's infinite wisdom go exactly where it is needed most, should it be for their higher good. May we all be empowered by your divine love and blessing – Amen."

You can of course create a completely different invocation, or simply let the words come to you on a session-by session basis. Your intuition will guide you and the most important thing is infusing your intention with love! And if there are specific areas where you want healing to be focused, such as a set injury or disease, you can add in the intention to work on these problem areas to your invocation. By adding in the disclaimer 'should it be for their higher good,' we are releasing control over the session and handing over the permission to the animal, to choose to accept the energy and partake in the session.

SCANNING THE BODY

You may choose to start a hands-on session by scanning the animal's whole body, holding your hands just above the body, to detect any signals or sensations that suggest a certain area may be in need of Reiki. This technique, known as Byosen Reikan Ho, allows you to harness your own Reiki intuition to tailor the animal's Reiki session to their needs.

To scan the body, you can start by holding your hands about six inches above the animal's body and running your hands through their aura from the top to the bottom of their body. You can check for any energy blockages or hot spots that you can work on during the Reiki session.

Notice any colors, vibrations or any sensations in your hands. Repeat this motion for a further two times to help harmonize or 'cleanse' their aura and remove any superficial energy build ups. This gentle and peaceful exercise also helps to build trust and rapport with the animal.

The more you practice this technique, the more you will develop your intuitive ability to detect fluctuations in energy. Trust what you feel and sense – this is your natural Reiki instinct at work!

UNDERSTANDING THE SIGNS THAT AN ANIMAL IS ACCEPTING REIKI

"Thousands of candles can be lighted from a single candle, and the life of the candle will not be shortened. Happiness never decreases by being shared." – Buddha

Every animal has its own personality and behaviors, for this reason every animal will respond differently to a Reiki session. There are a number of additional factors that will affect how an animal responds to Reiki. These include whether you are a stranger or known to the animal, how often the animal meets new people, whether it has experienced abuse or neglect as well as whether it is currently suffering from an illness or any discomfort.

There are however, tell-tell signs that an animal is receiving and comfortable accepting Reiki, these include:

- Moving closer to your hands, even pushing their body into them
- Licking or smelling your hands
- Sustained eye contact
- Lying down near you
- Deep sighing
- Yawning
- Falling asleep
- Moving their bodies to direct your hands somewhere
- Push the area of the body where they are having issues up to your hands for healing.

But what will the animal feel during a session?

Like humans, there are some commonalities in what we expect animals to feel during a session – but again these will be unique to each animal. These include:

- Feeling a warmth or a chill spread over their body
- Becoming very relaxed and calm
- Becoming tired, falling asleep (otherwise known as a 'Reiki nap') or yawning
- Seeing colors more vividly
- A gentle buzzing or tingling
- Flashes of memories

- Flashes of past life experiences
- Involuntary movements or mild spasms
- Pins and needles
- Itchiness
- Rumbling stomach
- Feeling at peace
- Feeling happier or the urge to cry as emotional blockages are lifted

Healing Reactions

Although rare, some animals can experience what are known as 'healing reactions' where their current symptoms or new ones arise as part of the detoxification and healing process. For example, if a pet has a skin condition, they may start itching intensely during or after the Reiki treatment. Or if you are working with animal with specific behavioral or emotional problems their reactions may be briefly intensified after the session.

Just like a cold where the symptoms sometimes get worse before getting better, these healing reactions are temporary as the animal's body begins to rebalance itself in order to facilitate the natural healing of the ailment or illness. Continuing Reiki treatments with the animal will help to work through these reactions.

Remember although Reiki is 100% safe and natural and cannot do any harm, if your animal has a reaction that you are concerned about, you should always contact your vet immediately.

USING HAND POSITIONS DURING AN ANIMAL REIKI SESSION

"If having a soul means being able to feel love and loyalty and gratitude, then animals are better off than a lot of humans." — James Herriot

A great way to start a hands-on Reiki session is with your hands open on your lap or by your sides, so the animal can sense the Reiki energy and decide whether they are comfortable with a hands-on treatment. If the owner and animal have given permission, you can use a series of hand positions which will help you to access the animal's charka points. Remember Reiki energy will always go where it is needed and you don't need to use any set hand positions to work with an animal- some people just prefer to work through the chakras in full or focus in on one chakra using these positions. It's simply your preference.

Don't forget, if you are going to be touching the animal, make sure you do so very softly and that your hands are warm. The hands should be cupped slightly with fingers together to concentrate the flow of energy and to stop energy dissipating through your fingers. As you work on a chakra, you can visualize opening up this energy center just as you would open a door, letting pure white energy flow through into the chakra and wash over the animal. We will work through the chakras from the head to the feet of the animal, using a dog to demonstrate how to access the chakras.

It's important to note here, that a lot of animals don't like being touched on their face or head, so whilst we will work through the hand positions from the head of the animal, we find it's often better to begin a session by working on the body of the animal at the shoulder blades or chest. Once the animal becomes more comfortable with the energy and noticeably relaxes, perhaps positioning their head near your hands or falling asleep, you can then move your hands back to their head.

- The Head – Touch or hover cupped hands over the top of the animal's head. Visualize opening the Crown Chakra and energizing the area with love and your healing intention. Stroking the top of the animal's head between their ears is one of the ways you can treat this chakra.

- The Eyes – The Third Eye Chakra is located between the eyes in the middle of the forehead, we can move our hands from the Crown to the sides of the animal's face over their eyes. However, we never touch the animal's eyes.

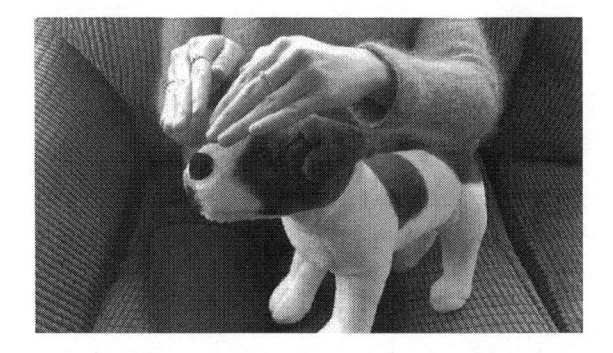

- The Ears – Most animals don't like their ears being touched, however if you are able to get close to their ears, hovering your hands a short distance over them will allow you to work with the Minor and Bud Chakras controlling the sensory systems in the animal.

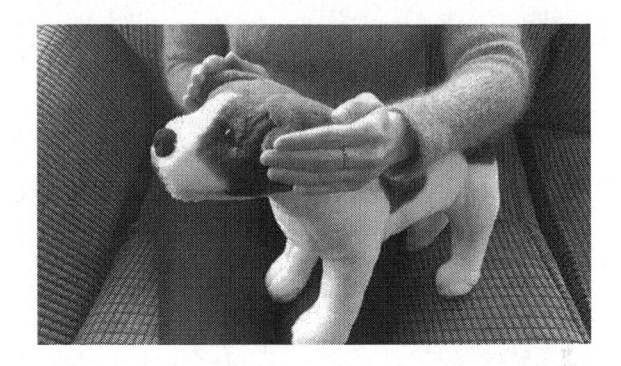

- The Neck – To work on the Throat Chakra, touch or hover one hand on the throat and the other hand on the back of the neck. Alternatively, you can stroke the back of the neck.

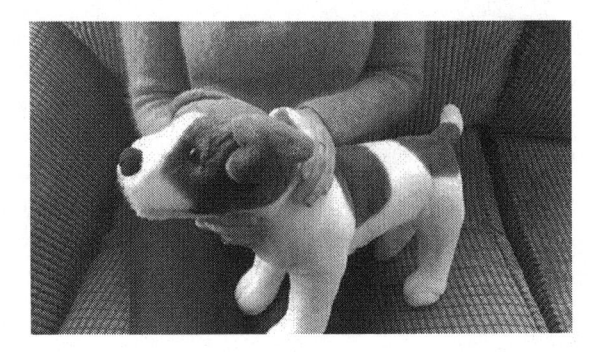

- The Chest or Shoulder Blades – Continue to the chest of the animal for the Heart Chakra. You can treat the front and the back of the chest at the same time with one hand on the chest and one hand on the shoulders. Some animals don't like their front being touched. If this is the case, you can place both of your hands on their shoulder blades – allowing Reiki to flow to the chest and down the front limbs. You may equally want to place one hand on the shoulder blades and one hand on the hips to work across the back of the animal. As mentioned, we find that these positions are well received by animals that we work with and are often the best place to start a session.

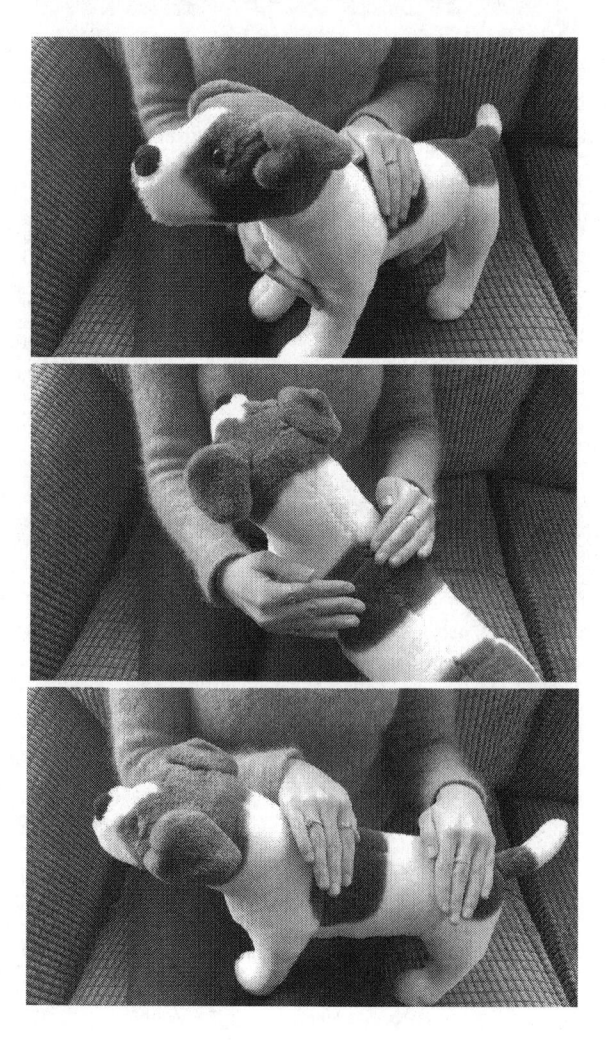

- The Stomach – Continue to the stomach/abdominal region where the Solar Plexus Chakra can be treated. Again, depending on how sensitive and accessible this area is, you can cup the belly with your hand or hover one hand near the stomach at the front of the body, with the other hand in the middle of their back.

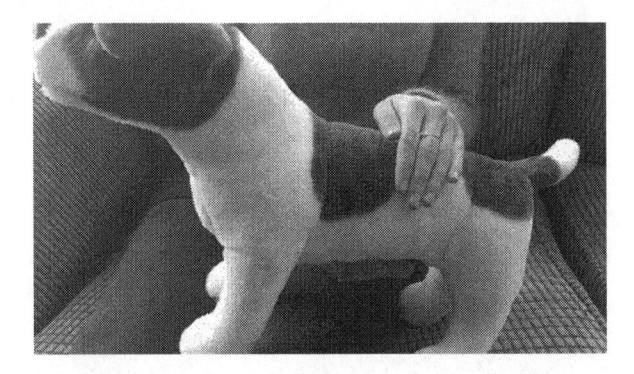

- The Hip Area/Lower back and Tailbone – Continue to work down the body to the hips. For the Sacral Chakra place your hands on or above the hips or the animal's flanks, then moving to the lower back and hind/tailbone area for the Root Chakra.

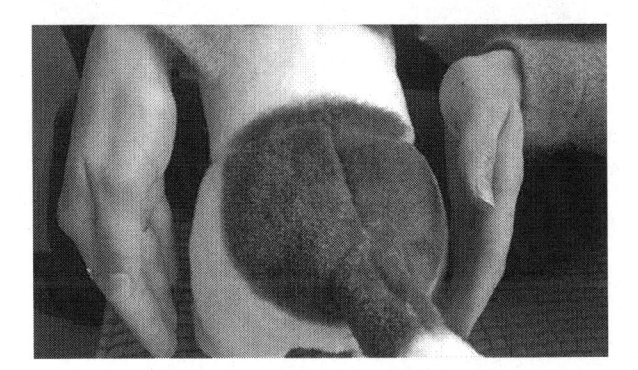

- The Leg joints – Cup or hover the hands over the leg joints if this is comfortable for the animal and it is safe for you to get close to the legs. You can alternatively channel Reiki down through the legs from the last position working on the tailbone area as we known bone and joint issues can be very sensitive.

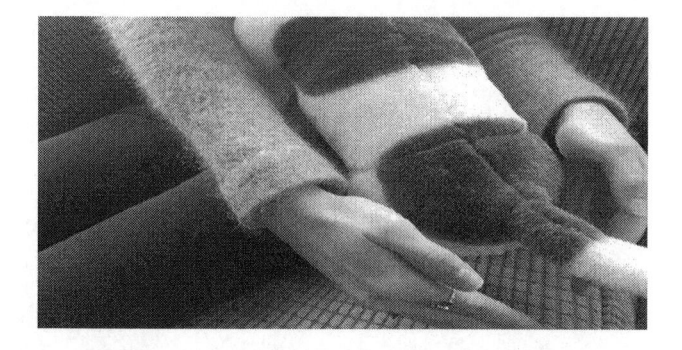

- The Feet – The paw pads can be very sensitive, so again hover your hands over or beam Reiki to these areas.

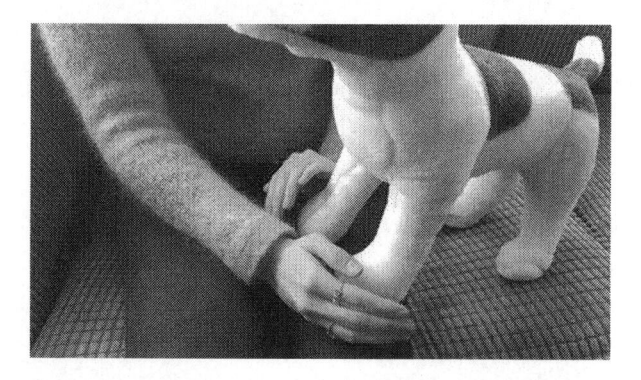

When you have finished treating the animal, visualize the pure white light running through their whole body in a continuous stream and begin to end the session.

If you are aware of any issues the animal is experiencing, you may want to focus time on this area or body system but just remember Reiki will work to treat the whole animal from any position, not just certain symptoms or issues.

WHY THE HAND POSITIONS ARE ONLY A GUIDE

Whilst many animals will happily settle into a session with you to get the energy they need during a treatment, it would be unrealistic to assume that every animal will lie or sit down in exactly the right position whilst you perform every hand position in order, or even that you would want to make the animal do so. Subsequently, there is a bigger element of improvisation and more flexibility required when working with animals.

Animals move about, they fidget, they want to play, they get distracted easily and do whatever they want in that moment. They may make it very clear that they do not want a treatment, shift constantly between wanting hands-on Reiki and wanting you to proceed at a distance, or just completely walk away and end a treatment early – they do what's best for them. They want to feel in control just like we would when faced with a new experience.

Some areas of the animal's body will be sensitive or too difficult to access if they are constantly moving about, so you should always start with your hands a short distance from the body.

The important thing is that there is no wrong way to perform Reiki. You could complete all hand positions, maintain one or two hand positions during the whole treatment or move to a certain area to focus healing towards one ailment.

Depending on whether the animal is lying down, sitting or standing, you may have to adapt the hand positions as you never want to move an animal to complete them. So, if the animal does relax into one position during the treatment, try not to move your hands in a way that will disturb them. Some animals may be uncomfortable with two hands close to them, so working with one hand on their body whilst the other remains on your lap or by your side may help them relax. Alternatively, the animal may respond better to your hands if you use one to lightly stroke, rub or lightly scratch the animal during the treatment until they are more at ease.

As animals are more sensitive to energy than humans, working through several different positions for a long period of time may be too intense, so working chakra by chakra may not be necessary. Unless they are very ill, they may only need a little Reiki energy.

These hand positions are only a guide, and whilst they may work well with cats, dogs and other small animals where you can work with the animal on your lap or close by, they may not suit all species. For some small animals such as mice and birds you may be able to fit the whole animal in the palms of your hands! In these cases, you may wish to cup the animal in your hands as you channel Reiki or hover your hands over the whole animal and use visualization to channel Reiki through the energy systems. For larger animals like horses, you may find it more difficult to reach all the different chakra points, or it may not be safe to do so if you are unfamiliar with horses. Again, you can work on the whole energy system by beaming Reiki or by sending Reiki distantly as you progress as a Reiki Practitioner. Just because you can't touch an area doesn't mean Reiki won't go there. Reiki is wise and will go where it needs to.

HAND POSITIONS AND INTUITION

Intuition is something that we are all familiar with in everyday life, sometimes you just instinctively know, feel or understand something. Following your Reiki Intuition is an important part of Reiki mastery.

Many Reiki masters use their intuition to guide hands-on treatments, allowing Reiki to direct their hands to the area where energy is needed. Indeed, you may notice that Reiki's subtle energies will begin to steer your treatments to maximize the benefits for the animal. This is usually in the form of knowing where to focus your energy, exactly where to place your hands in each hand position and knowing when to move on to the next hand position.

Your hands are really your compass and guide in terms of knowing what to do during a Reiki session. You may feel a tingling sensation, an itch or pain, a magnetic pull or heat in your hands as they move over an area, or sense energy being pulled through your hands. Sometimes your hands will move on their own. Changes in these sensations will also help you know when to stop and move on to another position, or you may receive another intuitive message to move on. You can use a set number of breaths as a guide at each position if you do not get any intuitive guidance. (Remember just because you can't feel or sense something doesn't mean Reiki isn't working).

It is important to also listen to the animal's energies and non-verbal cues – they may sigh deeply or move themselves to a different position where they want Reiki energy to flow. If they don't like a certain position, they will show you and prompt you to move on – be responsive to these cues. Likewise, if the animal wants you to touch them directly, they will move into your hands. You should never assume that an animal will be comfortable with hands-on healing even if you've used this method with them before. If they move away, assess the energy flow and end the treatment if necessary.

HOW DO YOU KNOW WHEN TO END AN ANIMAL REIKI SESSION?

"Every animal knows more than you do." - Native American Proverb

Just like human Reiki sessions can vary in nature and length of time, no two animal Reiki sessions will ever be the same, even with the same animal. Depending on the needs and size of the animal, you could feel them pulling back from Reiki within 5 to 10 minutes or they may work with you for a whole hour. Both outcomes are totally normal, and it really is dependent on what the animals wants. When the session is drawing to a close, it is normal to feel the flow of Reiki energy begin to trickle off and stop.

Over time you will be able to recognize the types of behaviors and body language that an animal will present when they are ready for a session to end. These can include the animal stretching or getting up and wandering off or becoming uninterested in the session – they may resume normal activities like eating or playing or focused on something new.

If you are working with an animal that doesn't show any obvious changes in their behavior throughout the treatment, you can look to yourself for the right signs to end the session. You may sense the energy flow through your hands weaken or find yourself suddenly very alert, leaving your meditative state.

When you are ready to bring a Reiki session to a close, firstly make sure you thank the animal for the experience that you have shared. You may also want to say a little prayer or send your blessings to the animal for their health and wellbeing. You can do this either aloud or in your own heart and mind.

Aura cleansing at the end of the session is a good way the 'seal in' the work that you have done, balancing the animal's energy systems.

Next, we advise closing yourself down so that you are no longer being used as a channel for Reiki. This doesn't mean you are no longer connected to the Universal Life Force – but instead signifies that you are ending the healing session. To close down, ensure your feet are on the floor (either sitting or standing) and imagine a white light of pure, positive energy moving down through your body from head to toe. As it passes through your chakras, visualize these closing like doors. When the light has reached the ground, you will be closed down. One other technique to close down, is to visualize physically cutting the energy connection between you to the animal, and then surrounding yourself in pure white light. Washing your hands after a session is another useful grounding technique.

The animal may wish to show you their appreciation at the end of the Reiki session in a number of unique ways. These could include:

- Flicking or wagging their tail
- Appearing excited or animated
- Making happy sounds (nickering, purring etc.)
- Placing their paw on your body
- Friendly licks
- Nuzzling their head on your body

- If they are asleep or relaxed, just let them stay where they are comfortable and try your best not to disturb them as you leave.

You may want to take a few minutes to note down anything that you experienced during the session. If you are working on someone else's animal, you may want to speak to the owner after the session to let them know anything you observed during the treatment. (But remember you are not there to diagnose or advise on the animal's health.) Its best to only generally comment on what you experienced such as mentioning that you concentrated your healing on a certain part of the body or that you noticed that there were some energy blockages when working through the treatment. If they have further questions, it's important to emphasize that you cannot ever fully understand the root of the issues – you are only there to channel Reiki and the session you have worked through can only do good.

Few people get to connect to animals in the way Reiki Masters can, and you should respect the private connection you have shared with the animal whenever it is appropriate and beneficial to the animal. If you feel that the animal would benefit from further sessions, you would speak to the guardian to schedule in the appointments, and just remind the owner of the need to help the animal through any energy detoxing –making sure they are hydrated and get the rest, exercise and nutrition they need, where applicable.

As you are not utilizing your own energy reserves when channeling Reiki, you shouldn't feel drained after a session. However, it is important to take some time to relax and restore your energy if you do feel drained after any Reiki treatments. Work through your meditation exercises, visualizing yourself being surrounding by a protective and loving white light.

DIFFERENT ANIMALS WILL HAVE DIFFERENT NEEDS

"For an animal person, an animal-less home is no home at all." — Cleveland Amory

We have spoken a lot about how you must always cater an animal Reiki session to the specific needs and temperament of the animal, making sure both you and the animal are safe and comfortable.

Let's take a little look at some of the different considerations for working with different animal species!

REIKI WITH DOGS

"A dog represents all that is best in man." -
Etienne Charlet

Reiki can be used to help dogs in a number of ways. Many people turn to Reiki to help their dog recover from an accident or operation, or to help with common species-specific conditions like arthritis and joint pain, heart issues, ear infections and breathing difficulties. Dogs are highly intelligent social beings and can develop behavioral issues and emotional problems such as separation anxiety and aggressive tendencies if they don't get the training, support or contact they need to thrive. So Reiki can help with many social and behavioral issues too.

But Reiki isn't just for when things go wrong – it is a great way to maintain a dog's health and wellbeing just like a natural supplement can support their dietary needs. Whatever the breed, size or age of the dog, Reiki can help a dog's physical, mental and emotionally health.

When working with dogs it's important to be aware of their sociable nature and emotional demands. When they enter new environments or meet new people or animals, they are naturally inquisitive so they like to investigate, sniff and bark and may get excited or nervous. This is why it is important to work in an environment that they are already very comfortable with, and also that you start a session feeling calm and composed. If they get excited and try and play with you when you first greet them, just try to stay calm and still and let them familiarize themselves with you. They should eventually relax into the session once they acknowledge your intention and trust your energy.

There may be times where you may not be able to work with the animal in their home or a familiar environment. In such cases, it's better to build trust with the animal first so they are at least comfortable with you and your intentions - remaining calm, collected and peaceful is key. Over time, particularly if you have had a few sessions with an animal, they will often feel more at ease around you.

Dogs are creatures of habit and seem to instinctively know when it's time to eat or go for a walk. At these times they will tend to be focused solely on eating or walking, and often become overexcited in anticipation. We would recommend avoiding a Reiki session directly before these times for this reason. This is particularly important when meeting and working with the animal for the first time. It's best to find a time when they dog is most relaxed and settled. If you are working with someone else's dog, the owner should be able to advise you on when this is, as they will be familiar with their dog's temperament throughout the day.

When treating a dog, there are several options for approaching the treatment, utilizing either hands-on, beaming or distant Reiki. Every session will vary to reflect the needs of the dog and how they want to accept Reiki.

- Whilst friendly calm animals may settle down by you very quickly and accept hands-on Reiki, more active and very playful animals may prefer to move around the treatment space.
- Anxious, skittish dogs will prefer less contact and may need more distant sessions.
- Shelter animals or rescue dogs who have been mistreated or abused are more likely to respond negatively to human contact, so again you will need to work at a distance from the animal.
- Aggressive or dangerous animals will need to remain on a lead or in a cage and should always be treated at a distance with a protective barrier between you and the animal.
- Smaller dogs may be used to sitting on their owners' laps and may be comfortable on your lap.
- If the dog is very big and there is a chance they may knock you over if you sit on the floor with them, you may want to sit on a chair to work through the session.

Some dogs may be very nervous and reluctant to leave their owner's side and you will need to work with the owner to find the best way to treat the animal. Due to the close connection dogs form with their guardians, you may feel the need to treat the owner with Reiki as well, as the dog may be harboring or mirroring emotional issues from their caretakers.

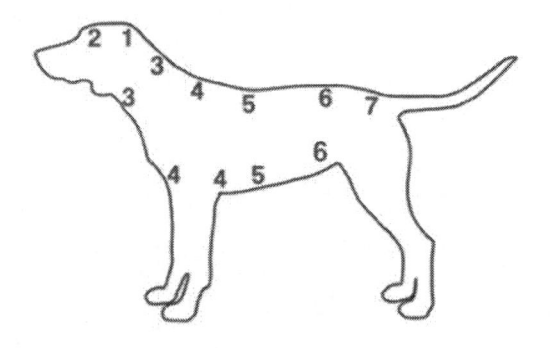

Chakras

1. Crown Chakra
2. Third Eye Chakra
3. Throat Chakra
4. Heart Chakra
5. Solar Plexus Chakra
6. Sacral Chakra
7. Root Chakra

REIKI WITH CATS

"Way down deep, we're all motivated by the same urges. Cats have the courage to live by them."
- Jim Davis

As cats are very independent animals you should never put any pressure on a cat to accept Reiki in any way. This means that you should always start a session with ample distance between you and the cat in order to give them the option to approach you if they wish. Let the cat decide how they would like to share Reiki and adapt the session to suit their disposition and personality. Working with a cat at a time when they are most relaxed will also help to set the right mood for the session.

The most common ways to conduct a Reiki session with a cat include:

- Working with the cat close to you or sitting on your lap if the cat is your own or very comfortable with you.
- If you don't know the cat well, start at a distance and they will come to you if they want to. You can sit or stand in the same room as the cat, with the cat either free to roam around the room or inside a crate (the kind that they use when being transported to the vets can work quite well).

- You can of course also work distantly using distant Reiki – you may be in another room to the cat or a different location all together. This is appropriate for cats who are prone to aggressive behavior or if they are particularly nervous or mistrusting of humans, or if you simple cannot get to see the cat due to distance. It goes without saying that you should always work with a cat in a crate or with a barrier between you and the animal if you are weary or unsure of their disposition.

If the cat is your own pet, then many people like to start a session by carrying out a self-treatment whilst meditating in a room that the cat can access. You can focus on channeling energy through your whole body allowing it to radiate out to fill the room and anyone that enters. This will allow the cat to familiarize itself with the energy and approach you if they would like a more focused treatment. Repeating this method over a few days will enable to cat to relax around the energy and become more receptive to accepting it.

When working with a cat that is not your own, you can adapt this method to create a relaxed environment for Reiki. Start by finding a comfortable position in the same room as the cat, but make sure you are a considerable distance from them. Begin to meditate, connecting to Reiki with the intention to provide relaxation and healing if the car wishes to receive it. Communicate to the cat that they can draw as much or as little Reiki energy through you as they want – they are in complete control.

Most cats will prefer to remain at a distance, eventually settling nearby. They may lay by your side, rub up against you or even approach you and sit on your lap. If they climb onto your lap or chest and start to purr, then you can slowly transition to hands-on Reiki. Stroking the cat is a good way to start channeling Reiki into their body, and you may want to continue stoking them throughout the session as a means of comfort. If they don't respond well to stroking but remain close, you can place your hands a few inches above their body.

Be aware that some cats will relax and fall asleep but always remain at a distance – this is fine, you can continue to beam Reiki across the room and should not try to get closer. They also may move back and forth throughout the session. If this is the case, just keep the channel open and focus on the intent to support the cats healing needs in the best way possible.

If the cat doesn't want to accept Reiki, you can still connect to Reiki but set the intention to allow the animal to receive the energy at a time that suits them.

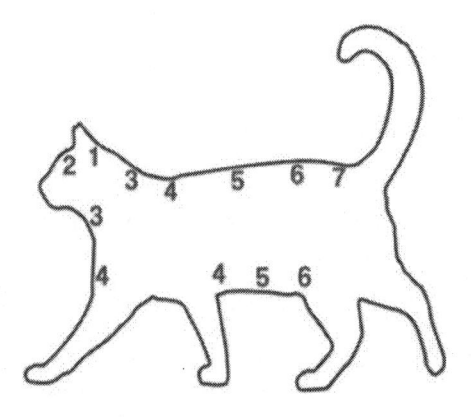

Chakras

1. Crown Chakra
2. Third Eye Chakra
3. Throat Chakra
4. Heart Chakra
5. Solar Plexus Chakra
6. Sacral Chakra
7. Root Chakra

REIKI WITH BIRDS

"Everyone likes birds. What wild creature is more accessible to our eyes and ears, as close to us and everyone in the world, as universal as a bird?" -
David Attenborough

Birds are becoming increasingly popular family pets owing to their vibrant personalities and sociable nature. The make great companions as they thrive on interaction with their owners, some singing and talking back. Common pet birds include cockatiels, parrots, budgies and canaries.

When treating a bird with Reiki it's important to understand their natural instincts and behaviors. As they are very intelligent social beings, they need daily interaction and mental stimulation to support their emotional health. They often form close bonds with humans or other birds and animals that they live with. This means they can get quite jealous and upset if other people interact with their family unit or if they lose a companion.

We also must empathize with these naturally free animals – flying is part of who they are. Even if they grow up in a domestic environment, they still need time to fly out of their cages or within a large aviary. As a result, birds can get very distressed and frustrated if they are unable to fulfil this innate need to fly, and these frustrations can lead to bad behavior such as loud screeching or self-destructive habits like feather-picking.

When we appreciate a bird's natural desires it's easier to understand how we can use Reiki to relax the animal and heal any emotional or mental imbalances, sending Reiki to difficult situations or strained relationships. Birds are very sensitive to Reiki and it can help to support their general wellbeing and develop more positive relationships in the bird's home.

If the bird typically lives in a cage, you can either start the session with the bird inside their cage or with the door to the cage left open so that they can fly free if they wish. We would always recommend leaving the birdcage in the room it's normally in, so that the bird feels most at ease with its surroundings.

If the bird lives within an aviary you can perform the whole Reiki session standing outside of the aviary, but be aware that if there are multiple birds inside you may find that other birds also pick up on the healing energy and desire a treatment as well. If it is an aviary within someone's home or garden, and the birds are used to being handled, the owner may suggests bringing the bird into a space on its own such as a living room. This is perfectly fine also.

Always begin at a distance in a position that is comfortable for you, whether that be sitting or standing. Start to connect to Reiki with your hands either at your side or on your lap. As the energy begins to flow through your hands, ask the bird's permission to work with them. You can then start the session by flooding the whole room with Reiki energy, allowing the Reiki to surround the bird. Move your focus to their cage and beam Reiki to remove any negative energy or stagnant issues from the bird's immediate environment. Then, if the bird invites you to do so, channel Reiki to the bird by visualizing peace and contentment, positive relationships and that beautiful feeling of freedom. Talking to the bird throughout the session will provide further comfort as they relax into the treatment.

There are several ways in which you can tell a bird is happy and comfortable accepting Reiki energy: they may approach you or your hands when you begin the session, give you lots of eye contact as if they are trying to figure you out, make happy chirping noises or talk to you, bob or bow their head, flap their wings as if they are trying to fly on the spot or rub or nuzzle up against you.

Typically, after a period of engagement with you, the bird will relax and remain calm and still. Some may even fall asleep. Every bird's reaction will be unique and may vary session to session.

You shouldn't attempt to wrap your hands around the bird or put any pressure on their body, remember they are small and fragile. Birds also don't usually like their back being touched.

If a bird has settled on your hands it's best to hold this position throughout the treatment, giving the bird the freedom to move away and come back at any time in the session. As birds are quite small, we don't work through the hand positions on them, however you can mentally send Reiki to each of their chakras without moving your hands. Equally you can focus on channeling Reiki into their body from the spot closest to your hands, with the intention that Reiki will spread through their body and go where it is needed.

Beaming is the method we most commonly use when working with birds, especially when the bird is going to be staying within their birdcage or aviary. It allows you to beam Reiki energy to them in a location where they feel comfortable.

As with all animals, when you start to sense the energy flow decreasing it means that the bird is pulling away from the session and doesn't want to receive any more Reiki at that time. You will know they are ready to end the treatment if they leave their relaxed and calm state and start to return to their normal activities such as singing, drinking or flying about.

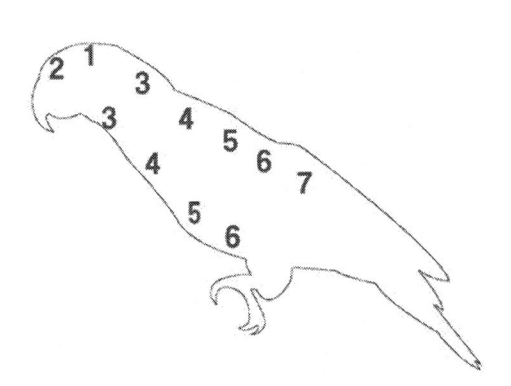

Chakras

1. Crown Chakra
2. Third Eye Chakra
3. Throat Chakra
4. Heart Chakra
5. Solar Plexus Chakra
6. Sacral Chakra
7. Root Chakra

REIKI WITH HORSES

*"The earth would be nothing without the people,
but the man would be nothing without the horse."*
– Unknown

The history between horses and humans is a long one. Horses were domesticated by humans thousands of years ago – they have been put to work in various occupations and have become cherished companions. They are one of the earths most majestic creatures and their partnership with humans is a gift.

Although you may ride or work with one horse on its own, naturally horses are herd animals. Their survival in the wild would depend on the relationships they form with the other horses in their herd – with dominant horses leading the group and the rest of the herd accepting their position under the leader. Horses are confident, intelligent, energetically sensitive animals, that quickly pick up and respond to human energy. They can sense nervousness and fear and will flee when they believe they are in any risk of danger. As a result, staying calm and composed around a horse is very important – and this applies to Reiki Practitioners working on a horse or herd.

As we have stressed before, unless you know the animal well, we always advise starting a Reiki treatment from a distance, and this can be especially true for horses as not everyone has experience and confidence working with them. You should only ever work close to a horse when you feel completely safe and confident, but still start the session about fifteen feet away from the horse and give them the space to move about during the treatment and get used to the energy.

There are a number of reasons why horse owners seek out Reiki. Reiki is one way to work with stressed or unhappy horses, allowing the animal to release emotional anxiety and frustration and also let go of bad experiences or memories from any incidences in their past. In their natural environment horses would gallop freely, so it is understandable that horses may become stressed, anxious and frustrated when they are kept enclosed for considerable periods of time. Some owners turn to Reiki to help their horse with physical problems such as an old injury that is affecting their legs, or alternatively if need help with a misbehaving or anxious horse acting up in their stable or during grooming. If it is a working horse, whether that be farm work or competing in various equestrian competitions, an owner may seek your help with a specific work-related enquiry, for example a horse that becomes nervous when travelling in a horse box to attend events.

If you are working with a horse that has an owner or is in some form of domesticated arrangement, it is common to carry out the session whilst they are in their stable or in a paddock, or when they are safely tied to a familiar structure. This a great fit for a Reiki session as the horse is in an environment that they know well, and you can practice Reiki comfortably knowing that there is a barrier between you and the horse. If you do not know the horse, you should continue to work at a distance throughout the session either beaming Reiki across the stable or paddock or using distant healing to channel Reiki across a larger distance. You should always keep a big enough distance between yourself and the horse that if they do move suddenly you wouldn't be in harm's way and you could get away if you needed to.

Once you have greeted the horse, ask their permission to enter their space and work with them – reaffirming that they can draw as much energy through you as they see fit. Connect to Reiki and set the intention to surround the horse with loving healing energy, adding in any specific healing needs.

If you are working on a horse you know well and feel confident to attempt hands-on Reiki, we advise that you still start from a distance and allow them to walk over to you for Reiki healing. We recommend you only proceed if you have experience working with horses, and only work with the horse from the front or side of their body to begin with as standing behind the horse or close to its legs may put you in danger.

You may find yourself intuitively drawn to a certain area and you should always follow your intuition. Scanning the horse's aura may flag some problem areas you want to focus on, or equally the horse may lead your hands by turning their body to meet them. During a hands-on treatment the horse will usually relax and may remain still as you move your hands along their body, or similarly keep peacefully grazing.

Some horses may come and go throughout the session or begin to relax at a distance from you. If the horse does move away, give them the space they need and continue working from a distance if appropriate. You can work through the horse's energy systems using your intention and visualization to channel energy to the horse.

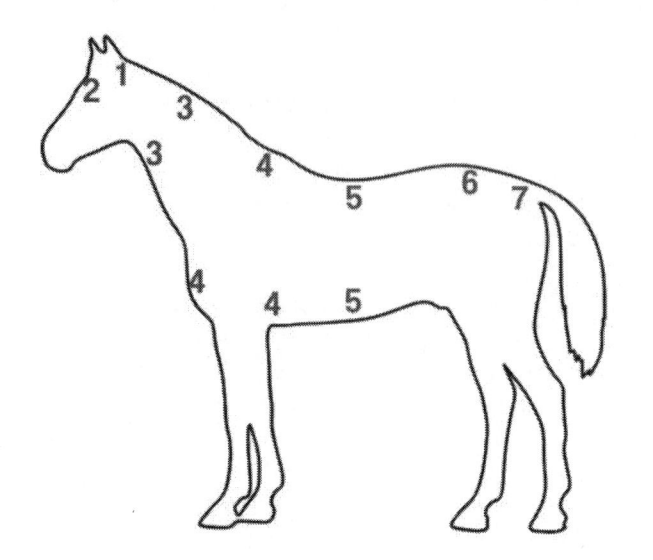

Chakras

1. Crown Chakra
2. Third Eye Chakra
3. Throat Chakra
4. Heart Chakra
5. Solar Plexus Chakra
6. Sacral Chakra
7. Root Chakra

REIKI WITH OTHER SMALL ANIMALS

"If a man aspires towards a righteous life, his first act of abstinence is from injury to animals." - Albert Einstein

It's not just dogs and cats that make fantastic companions – many people care for other small animals like hamsters, rabbits, gerbils and mice in their home. Not all our pets are furry either – tortoises, lizards, spiders and snakes are all cherished pets. And we must not forget our aquatic family members – most of us have probably had a pet fish at some point in our lives!

Due to their size, small animals are very sensitive to Reiki energy. For this reason, we always start a Reiki treatment from a distance. Touching them directly with hands-on Reiki can be very intense and overwhelming for the animal and in turn, they may reject the healing which is not what we want. They may be nervous around humans they don't know simply because of just how large we are compared to them!

It's certainly important to be aware of your own strength when working with small animals. A stroke on the back that would be an acceptable pressure for a cat or dog won't be OK for a hamster or lizard. It's best to just assume smaller animal = more fragile!

Some people aren't very comfortable around some smaller, more atypical pets like spiders, snakes or rats. If this is you, don't worry! You are the only person that can judge which animals you feel comfortable working with. Remember animals can pick up on anxiety or nervousness so if you have arachnophobia it's best not to work with any spider clients. However, you may feel comfortable sending Reiki distantly to a friend's tarantula.

Most domestic small animals will live primarily within some form of enclosure, be it a hutch, cage, tank or vivarium. There is no need to take them out of their enclosures for a Reiki session, if this is where they usually live! Keeping them in their enclosure whilst you sit or stand a short distance away, gives them the freedom to move closer to you in their cage if they want to, whilst allowing them to relax as they can remain in an environment they know. Always work with an animal in its cage if you have any doubts or if the animal could bite you or injure you.

This is not to say that you can't work with a bunny rabbit on your lap for example, if they are very used to being near to you or stroked. In such occasions, you can either begin working at a distance but with the door to the enclosure open, or bring the rabbit into a space that they are used to, such as a living room, starting the session standing or sitting away from them. Depending on whether you are sitting or standing you can lay your hands on your lap or hold your hands by your side with your palms facing outwards. If the rabbit is comfortable with the Reiki energy you may find that they wander up to your legs to be closer to you and you can offer hands-on healing if you think it is appropriate.

And when it comes to pet fish, you can beam Reiki to the fish and the water in which they live. Indeed, water is the perfect medium for transmitting Reiki energy as it surrounds the fish and passes through their bodies as they swim and breath, allowing Reiki to flow through their body. What a special experience! We tend to start a session with a fish by setting the intention to infuse the tank or aquarium with Reiki energy, to balance the environment and allow positive healing energy to surround the fish. And then we will beam Reiki directly to the fish's body as well, visualizing the energy working to balance the fish's chakras and provide healing on all levels.

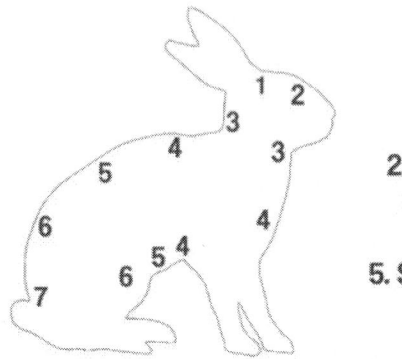

Chakras

1. Crown Chakra
2. Third Eye Chakra
3. Throat Chakra
4. Heart Chakra
5. Solar Plexus Chakra
6. Sacral Chakra
7. Root Chakra

GOOD LUCK ON YOUR REIKI JOURNEY

"Learning is the beginning of wealth. Learning is the beginning of health. Learning is the beginning of spirituality. Searching and learning is where the miracle process all begins." - Jim Rohn

There are a million different animal species on our planet, and we are surrounded by animal life, from our loving pets to the wildlife in our local area. In practicing Animal Reiki, you will find yourself more connected to all of the animal energies on the planet and in turn Mother Nature herself.

You will find that the more animals you begin to treat with Reiki, the more you will start to meet and interact with those who need Reiki healing. The opportunities with Reiki are endless and we encourage you to practice, further your study and spread the joy and loving power of Animal Reiki.

If you are looking to gain certification in Animal Reiki, you can complete our Animal Reiki Master Teacher online training course. This course includes your Reiki

Master Attunement Ceremony and extra learning materials and bonuses to help you progress!

For More Information about Reiki and our certified Reiki Home Study Courses please visit: www.reiki-store.com.

ABOUT THE REIKI STORE

"The journey of a thousand miles begins with one step." - Lao Tzu

It all started with a little purple Reiki Book, and a mission to help as many people as possible...

As one of the very first online Reiki schools, The Reiki Store, has remained a leading voice in holistic health community for over two decades. Founded by our parents Garry and Adele Malone in 1997, with the mission to make the power of Reiki energy accessible to everyone, we are a family-run training school that specializes in holistic training courses that improve health and wellbeing and are proud to have helped tens of thousands of students on their path to Reiki mastery.

Our Reiki courses are led by a team of accomplished Reiki Masters, Psychologists, Neurolinguistic Practitioners, Biologists and Mindfulness experts, all driven by a shared passion for helping as many people as possible live healthier, happier lives. We empower our students to reconnect with themselves and open their minds up to a more natural and holistic way of living.

In a noisy, demanding and stressful world, we strive to provide an online learning sanctuary that is grounded in balance, calm, wellness and mindfulness. Looking for answers and solutions from within ourselves and nature. We know that every person on this planet has a unique and incredible in-built power that can be used to affect positive change and believe that Reiki is a powerful way to unlock that inner strength and wisdom. Reiki can provide relaxation, pain-relief, improve our awareness and focus and help us be kinder to ourselves and those around us, including our pets!

Everything we do is about harnessing natural energy techniques and remedies to rebalance and recharge, promoting health on all levels – mind, body and spirit. We equip you with the skills you need to create positive habits and change in your life. Working with natural therapies and techniques that are good for you and the planet.

So whether you are training to become a Reiki Practitioner, or reading one of our books, newsletters or blogs we are very happy to welcome you to our community and hope this journey brings you the happiness, peace and love you deserve.

Find out more at www.reiki-store.com and follow us on our social channels to stay in touch.

Love and light,

The Reiki Store Family

Made in the USA
Columbia, SC
24 January 2025